HIMALAYAS

ABODE OF LIGHT

Portrait of Nicholas Roerich by Svetoslav Roerich

HIMALAYAS
ABODE OF LIGHT

NICHOLAS ROERICH

NICHOLAS ROERICH MUSEUM

NEW YORK   MMXVII

Nicholas Roerich Museum
319 West 107th Street
New York NY 10025
www.roerich.org

Cover illustration: Nicholas Roerich. *Mount of Five Treasures.* 1933

FIRST EDITION PUBLISHER'S NOTE

VISIONARY, master painter and world citizen, Nicholas Roerich is one of the outstanding personalities of this or any other century.

Unquestionably one of the most interesting and prolific of 20th century painters, his large canvasses run to the several thousands, each one a masterpiece of daring composition, glowing color harmony and massive effect. Himalayan is the word not only for his art, but also for his soul as well.

He was a daring pioneer as mystic, poet, thinker and scientist and his output as a writer was great and voluminous. From his mountain home in Kullu, India, he kept himself in touch with every progressive idea and movement in the outer world and often guided them with his wisdom and practical help.

His versatility is amazing; his capacity for work, prodigious. His interest in the small was as great and as enthusiastic as was his interest in the large. Whether painting a gorgeous Himalayan landscape or writing a short message to a school magazine, he gave it the same attention and care, a trait of true greatness.

India had a special place in his affection, and to India he looked for the spiritual regeneration of the world. Hence his home and retreat in the land of the Rishis. His great countrywoman and spiritual mentor, Madame Blavatsky, introduced him to India and to Indian wisdom, as she did to that other great Russian, Scriabin. One reveals the glories of the superhuman world through his canvasses, the other his immortal compositions.

"One of the great intuitive minds of the age" was the tribute paid to Roerich by Gorky, himself another immortal. And in this collection of essays, written about the Himalayan soul, his intuitive wisdom expresses itself as beautifully in his words as in his painting.

CONTENTS

HIMALAYAS	11
HEAVENLY GIFTS	12
TREASURE OF THE SNOWS	16
SACRED ASHRAMS	23
ASCENDING THE HEIGHTS	27
HIMALAYAN SONG	31
FROM KAILAS	33
URUSVATI	38
LEGENDS	42
IN HIS NAME	46
MYSTERIES	51
RISHIS	55
HIMALAYAN PROPHECIES	57
SHAMBHALA	64
ABODE OF LIGHT	70
KNOWLEDGE OF EXPERIENCE	75
SHAMBHALE LAM	81
SACRED LAND	94
FRONTIERS OF SHAMBHALA	110
SHAMBHALA—MONSALVAT	115
TIBET	117
LIGHT IN THE DESERT	121
MAITREYA	147
LEGEND OF THE STONE	164
SACRED SIGNS	169

ABODE OF LIGHT

A HIMALAYAN DIARY

HIMALAYAS

HIMALAYAS! Here is the Abode of Rishis. Here is Shambhala. Here resounded the sacred Flute of Krishna. Here proclaimed the Blessed Gautama Buddha. Here originated all Vedas. Here lived Pandavas. Here—Gessar Khan. Here—Aryavarta. Himalayas, Jewel of India. Himalayas, Treasure of the World. Himalayas, the sacred Symbol of Ascent.

Oh, Bharata the Beautiful! Let me send Thee my heart-felt admiration for all the greatness and inspiration which fill Thy ancient Wisdom, for Thy glorious Cities and Temples, Thy Meadows, Thy Deobans, Thy sacred Rivers and Majestic Himalayas!

HEAVENLY GIFTS

JOYFULLY, we followed all the news and articles about the glorious celebration of Sri Ramakrishna's centenary. How wonderful it was that, here on our confused and disturbed earth, there was such widespread devotional reverence and admiration! And this recognition of the Great Attainment came from various countries, from different peoples. All dedications to the Blessed Bhagavan were permeated with a profound love from the heart—which means that the Message of the Paramahamsa deeply touched the very soul of humanity.

People should rejoice at every manifestation, for in it is expressed the striving toward the Good. In this common bliss is contained a real Heavenly Gift that mankind should cherish above all ages and nations. Did not the Bhagavan himself, in his goodness, show the example of tolerance, of compassion? If people would only manifest more care and reverence for the heavenly sendings which continuously illumine our dark earthly life!

Heavenly gifts are always connected to human consciousness with lightning speed. Everything from the Highest, everything from Above, naturally directs human imagination toward Light, toward sparkling urgency. And so it is. The greatest realization can come like lightning, instantaneously. But yet another condition has to be recognized in our earthly understanding: in these high conceptions is revealed a heavenly language, for which we have but poor expressions in our earthly tongue.

If we gather all our conventional definitions around

the concept of Heavenly Gifts, it will be but a weak and limited expression of the Ineffable.

Only the Heart can give life to such expressions as solemnity, greatness, ecstasy, awe, joy. Without transfiguration through the Heart, all these lofty words are but dead sounds. Thus, it has been ordained since antiquity that the Highest Gifts should be reverently accepted and introduced with dignity into earthly life.

Love, too, is like lightning; but it must be informed and affirmed by full consciousness, or even this worthy feeling will be but a shimmering mirage.

Many epics tell of the sending of Heavenly Gifts into earthly surroundings. Such legends offset human light-mindedness and introduce an understanding of higher concepts into the consciousness.

Heavenly Gifts, if not introduced lovingly and with care into earthly life, will be as wings torn off, which, despite their magnificent beauty, are useless. But the Highest Will provides wings for blissful flights. Without a genuine ardent striving toward the spiritual, humans will forget about the wings which will become dusty with disuse. The God-sent magnificence will be changed into morbid grayness.

Stuffed birds with motionless spread wings always arouse a sad thought: the symbol of movement and flight has been stilled, and is thus condemned as worthless.

The cultivation of Heavenly Gifts in earthly conditions is a difficult science. Difficult, for it is born of labor, a science, for many experiments and tests preceded the Heavenly blossom unfolding, unharmed, and perfect in its predestined grandeur.

Not only are the rare chosen ones called upon for the blossoming of Heavenly Gifts on earth; every home can have a sacred garden into which the Heavenly Gifts are brought with great love, and surrounded by the highest offerings the human heart can render.

At times, people in their despair imagine that the Heavenly Gifts have ceased to flow. But they do not consider that their own eyes may not be able to discern the Invisible Light in the glare of the sunshine. Do people not take refuge from blissful rain under an umbrella? And do people not flee into shelter, even into dungeons, from purifying thunderstorms and from majestic waves of Light? Do people not try to make a small thing of the Greatest? How sad it is when Heavenly Gifts—these generous, beautiful treasures—are derided or locked up in the safe of a miser!

The deniers will invent all imaginable excuses in order to shift their own ignorance and rudeness to others. Little physical effort is needed to destroy a beautiful flower; in the same way, very little coarse force is needed to defile the highest Heavenly Gift. But if anyone will argue that this is already known, let us reply with the words of Vivekananda: "If you know what is good, then why don't you follow the Ordainments?" In these significant words thunders a direct challenge to all who violate and abase the Highest. And is this question today not most imperative?

If anyone will tell you that repetition is unnecessary, answer: "If something useful is not applied, one must reaffirm it!" A discussion of whether help should at all be rendered would be immoral; everyone will agree that one should always help. This means that if somewhere, something precious is being neglected, then one should endlessly reaffirm it as long as one's voice lasts. And if anyone sees that a humanitarian principle is violated by ignorance or malevolence, it is his duty to point this out, if he is secure in his understanding of the true values.

Heavenly Gifts are many and diverse. These beautiful helpers are sent to assist humanity generously and magnificently. The shower of Bliss is poured forth in benevolent generosity, but only drops of this treasure reach the earth. Yet, every thought about Heavenly Gifts strengthens the heart.... especially now, when human hearts are in such confusion and deep pain, one should strive toward the highest of healing agents—toward Heavenly Gifts.

> Thy benevolence fills
> My hands. In profusion it pours
> Through my fingers. I cannot
> Contain it. I am not able to distinguish
> The glowing streams of richness. Thy
> Benevolent wave pours through the hands
> Upon earth. I do not see who will gather
> The precious gems. The tiny sprays,
> Upon whom will they fall? If only I could
> Carry home the Heavenly Gift!

TREASURE OF THE SNOWS

THROUGHOUT Sikkim thunder the huge trumpets! For all it is a great, a solemn day. Let us go to the temple to see the Dances of the Great Day of Homage to Kanchenjunga.

From all parts of Sikkim, many people gather in their strange and varied attire. Here are the Sikkimese, in their short red garments and their conical, feathered hats; here are the sober Bhutanese, startlingly like Basques or Hungarians; here stand the red-turbaned people from Kham; you can see the small, round caps of the valiant Nepalese gurkhas; the people of Lhasa, in their Chinese-like long garments; the timid, quiet Lepchas, and many Sharpa people; all types of hill people from many parts come to pay homage to the Five Treasures of Kanchenjunga that point the way to the sacred city of Shambhala.

The trumpets roar. The drums beat. The crowd shouts and whistles. The protector of Sikkim enters in a huge red and gold mask with a short spear in his hand. Around the fountain, from which the sacred water is drawn each morning, the impressive protector of Sikkim turns in a slow, benevolent dance, completing his magic circles. In each monastery in Sikkim, at the same hour, this sacred dance of the protector is being performed. Finishing his role, the protector joins the picturesque line of musicians.

Again sound the trumpets and the roar of the crowd. Then the protectress emerges from the temple. As a Kali or Dakini, with skulls adorning her head and in dark garments, the deity outlines the same circle; after performing her invocation, she seats herself beside the protector.

Again the crowd shouts and cries. One by one the protectors of the Five Treasures of Kanchenjunga emerge. They are ready to fight for the holy mountain, because in its caves great treasures have been guarded for centuries. They are ready to guard the religion that is supported by the hermits who send their benevolent blessings from mountain depths. Radiant are the streamers on the garments of these guardians. They glisten as snows glowing in the rays of the sun. They are ready to fight. They are armed with swords and protected with round shields. The dance of the warriors begins, reminiscent of the dances of the Comanches of Arizona. The swords are brandished in the air; guns are fired. The population of Sikkim may rejoice, beholding how the treasures of Kanchenjunga are guarded. They may be proud—never yet has the rocky summit of this white mountain been conquered! Only exalted keepers of the mysteries, high Devas, know the path to its summit. The guardians finish their dance; they divide into two parties. In slow tread they march, intoning a long song in which they boast and bet. Each tells of his prowess: "I can catch the world without a horse!" -- None can withstand my sword!" -- My shield is strong!" Then follows the short dance of warriors. They pass into the temple. Both the protectors rise and again, after several encircling dances, enter the low door. The performance is over.

Now the power of Kanchenjunga is disclosed in another way. One sees bows and arrows in the hands of the people. The old joy of Sikkim—the ancient art of archery—is to be demonstrated. The targets are far off. But the hill men still know their noble art, and the arrows shall certainly reach the hearts of Kanchenjunga's enemies. The festival is over. The long giant trumpets are carried back into the temple; drums, gongs, clarionets and cymbals are silent. The doors of the temple are closed. This is not Buddhism; this is a homage to Kanchenjunga.

And when we see the beautiful snowy peak we understand the spirit of the festival, because veneration of beauty is the basis of this exalted feeling. The hill people feel

[17]

beauty. They feel a sincere pride in these incomparable snowy peaks, the world giants, in the clouds and the mists of the monsoon. Yet, are these not only a superb curtain before the great mystery beyond Kanchenjunga? Many beautiful legends are connected with this mountain.

Beyond Kanchenjunga are old menhirs of the great sun cult. Beyond Kanchenjunga is the birthplace of the sacred Swastika, sign of Fire. Now in the day of Agni Yoga, the element of Fire is again entering the spirit and all the treasures of the earth are revered. For the legends of heroes are dedicated not so much to the plains as to the mountains! All teachers journeyed to the mountains. The highest knowledge, the most inspired songs, the most superb sounds and colors were created on the mountains. On the highest mountain there is the Supreme. The high mountains stand as witnesses to the great Reality. Even the spirit of prehistoric humanity enjoyed and understood the greatness of the mountains.

Whoever beholds the Himalayas recalls the great meaning of Mount Meru. The Blessed Buddha journeyed to the Himalayas for enlightenment. There, near the legendary sacred Stupa, in the presence of all the gods, the Blessed One received his Illumination. In truth, everything connected with the Himalayas reveals the great symbol of Mount Meru, standing at the center of the world.

The ancient people of wise India discerned in the splendor of the Himalayas the smile of mighty Vishnu, who stands as a heroic, undefeated warrior armed with discus, mace, war-trumpet and sword. All the ten Avatars of Vishnu reached perfection near the Himavat. The most remote and the oldest of them is the Avatar Dagon, the man-fish who saved the forefather of the earthly race, Manu. As far back as the time of the first cataclysm, the flood, Burma remembers Dagon, and claims that the Dagoba dedicated to him is more than three thousand years old. Then came the Tortoise,—the pillar of heaven—which in the depths of the ocean of space assisted the great upheaval that endowed the earth with the radiant goddess Lakshmi. Then came the ponderous earthly Boar; then the unconquerable Nri-simha, the man-lion who saved Prahlâda from the wrath of his sinning father. The fifth Avatar, Vâmana the dwarf, triumphed over another king, Bali, who like Prahlâda's father tried to possess the throne of Vishnu. The sixth Avatar, bearing the name of Brahman, is the great warrior Parashurâma, said in the ancient scriptures to have annihilated the race of Kshatriyas. The seventh Avatar appeared as Râma, the mighty, beneficent king of India, extolled in the Râmâyana. The eighth Avatar is Krishna, the sacred shepherd, whose teaching is glorified in the all-embracing Bhagavad Gita. The ninth Avatar, the blessed Buddha, is the great Avatar predicted by Vishnu as the triumph of wisdom and the destruction of demons and sinners by their own Karma. Vishnu's tenth Avatar, not yet manifest, is the future Maitreya. A great horseman, savior of humanity, the Kalki Avatar shall appear riding on a white horse; resplendent, with his triumphant sword in hand, he will restore the pure law of righteousness and wise rule on earth.

The advent of the resplendent day-goddess, Lakshmi, Vishnu's bride, has ever gladdened the Indian heart even as do the Himalayan summits. Vishnu's second Avatar, the blue Tortoise, aided in stirring up the great ocean of space, indicated in the Mahâbharata, the Ramayana, and the Vishnu-purana. To restore to the three regions of earth, air and heaven their lost treasures, Vishnu commanded the Devas, sons of heaven, sons of fire, to join the dark demonic Asuras in stirring the cosmic ocean in order to create the sea of milk, or Amrita, the heavenly nectar of life. The glowing Devas came to the edge of the sea, which moved like the shining clouds of autumn. And with the help of the Great One, they uprooted the holy mountain to serve as a churning pole. The great serpent Ananta offered himself as a rope, and the mighty Vishnu, assuming the form of an immense Tortoise, made a pivot for the pole. The Devas held the tail of the serpent and the Asuras approached the head; and the great creative churning began. The first creation of this turbulent labor was the divine cow, and the fountain of milk is shown in the Vedas as a raincloud that conquered the drought. Then was manifested Varuni, Vishnu's crystallized radiance. Then came the Pârijâta, the source of all heavenly fruits. Afterwards, the moon rose and was possessed by Shiva. At this moment, conflagration and destructive fumes emitted by this process engulfed the earth and threatened the whole Universe. Then Brahmâ, the creator, arose and bid Shiva to manifest his power. Shiva, for the sake of all existing beings, swallowed the poison in self-sacrifice and became Nilakantha, the blue-throated. Dhavantari then appeared bearing the precious cup of Amrita. Hark and rejoice! After him came the radiant Lakshmi herself. Luminous, surrounded by her celestial attendants, glowing like a lustrous chain of clouds! At the same time, the gray rain clouds, powerful elephants of heaven, poured water over her from golden vessels. Amrita was manifested and the eternal battle over the treasure of the universe began. The Devas and Asuras clashed in battle; but the Asuras were vanquished and driven to Pâtâla, the gloomy recesses of the earth. Again joy and happiness came to the three worlds—the festival of gods and humankind.

* * *

As you ascend the peaks of the Himalayas and look out over the cosmic ocean of clouds below, you see the ramparts of endless rocky chains and the pearly strings of cloudlets. Behind them march the gray elephants of heaven, the heavy monsoon clouds. Is this not a cosmic picture that fills you with the understanding of some great creative manifestation? The mighty serpent in endless coils sustains the Milky Way. The blue Tortoise of heaven and stars without number are as diamond treasures of a coming victory. You recall the huge "Mendangs" in the Sikkimese range, with their stone seats used by the great hermits for meditation before sunrise; the great poet Milaraspa knew the strength of the hour before dawn, and in this awesome moment his spirit merged with the great spirit of the world, in conscious unity.

Before sunrise there comes a breeze, and the milky sea undulates. The shining Devas have approached the tail of the serpent and the great stirring has begun! The clouds collapse like shattered walls of a prison. Verily, the luminous god approaches! But what has occurred? The snows are red as blood. But the clouds collect in an ominous mist and all that was erstwhile resplendent and beauteous becomes dense and dark, shrouding the gore of battle. Asuras and Devas struggle; the poisonous fumes creep everywhere. Creation must perish. But Shiva, in self-sacrifice, has consumed the poison that threatened the world's destruction—he, the great blue-throated! Lakshmi arises from darkness, bearing the chalice of nectar. And before her radiant beauty, all the evil spirits of the night disperse. A new cosmic energy is manifest in the world!

Where can one have such joy as when the sun is upon the Himalayas, when the blue is more intense than sapphires, when from the far distance, the glaciers glitter as incomparable gems! All religions, all teachings, are synthesized in the Himalayas. The virgin of dawn, the Ushas of the ancient Vedas, is possessed of the same lofty virtues as the joyful Lakshmi. There can also be distinguished the all-vanquishing power of Vishnu. Formerly He was Nârâyana, the cosmic being in the depths of creation. Finally, He is seen as the god of the sun; at His smile, out of the darkness, arises the great goddess of happiness.

And may we not also notice the link between Lakshmi and Mâyâ, mother of Buddha? All great symbols, all heroes, seem to be brought close to the Himalayas as if to the highest altar, where the human spirit comes closest to divinity. Are not the shining starts nearer when you are in the Himalayas? A simple Sardâr in your caravan asks you, "But what is hidden beneath the mighty mountains? Why are the greatest plateaus in the Himalayas? Some treasures must be there!"

In the foothills of the Himalayas are many caves; it is said that from these caves, subterranean passages proceed far below Kanchenjunga. Some have even seen the stone door that has never been opened, because the date has not arrived. The deep passages lead to a splendid valley. You can realize the origin and reality of such legends when you are acquainted with the unsuspected formation in Himalayan nature, when you personally see how close together the glaciers and rich vegetation lie. The homage to Kanchenjunga from the simple people does not surprise you, because you see it not as superstition, but as a page of poetic folk-lore. The folk-reverence of natural beauty has its counterpart in the lofty heart of the sensitive traveler who, enticed by the inexpressible beauties here, is ever ready to exchange his city life for the mountain peaks. For him, this exalted feeling has much the same meaning as has the conquering dance of the guardian of the mountains and the bevy of archers who stand vigilant, ready to guard the beauty and treasures of Kanchenjunga.

Hail to unconquered Kanchenjunga! Swami Vivekananda said: "The artist is the witness who testifies to the beautiful. Art is the most unselfish form of happiness in the world."

Indeed, this is a splendid affirmation.

SACRED ASHRAMS

KAILAS, Manasarowar, Badrinath, Kedarnath, Trilok-nath, Ravalsar—these glorious gems of the Highest always fill the heart with blissful tremor. When we were yet a day's journey from Manasarowar the entire caravan became uplifted—thus far does the aura of the holy ashram extend.

Another vivid recollection arises on the path to Triloknath. A long line of Sadhus and Lamas stretches along this road—the old sanctuary, the site of pilgrimage and prayer. These pilgrims have met here from many different roads. Some, already completing their spiritual journeying, are walking along with a trident; some carry bamboo staffs; others are without anything, even clothing. And the snow of the Rohtang Pass is no impediment to them.

The pilgrims proceed, knowing that the Rishis and the Pandavas dwelt here. Here is the Beas or Vyas; here is Vyasakund—the place of the fulfillment of all wishes. Here, Vyasa Rishi compiled the Mahabharata.

Not in legend alone, but in reality did the great Rishis and the Pandavas live here. Their presence breathes life into the cliffs, which are crowned with glaciers, and into the emerald pastures, where the yaks graze, and into the caves and the roaring torrents. From here those spiritual calls were sent forth that humanity has heard throughout all ages. These calls are taught in schools; they have been translated into many languages—and this crystal of attainment has been stratified into the cliffs of the Himalayas.

"Where can one find words with which to praise the Creator, after seeing the incomparable beauty of the Himalayas?" sings the Hindu. Along the paths of the

Guru, along the peaks of the Rishi, along the mountain paths of the pilgrims of the spirit lies that treasure which no torrent of rain can wear away, nor any lightning turn to ashes. He who walks toward the Good is blessed on all paths. How touching are all the narratives that tell of the meeting of righteous ones of various nations. The tops of the deodars of the forest touch each other in the wind. Thus, everything that is of the highest meets without injury or harm. Time was when quarrels were settled by "one on one" combat and decisions were reached by a conference of chiefs. So do the deodars discuss matters among themselves. What a meaningful word: deodar—the gift of God. And this significant name is not without reason, for the resin of the deodar has healing powers. Deodar, musk, valerian, roses and other similar substances comprise the beneficent medicines of the Rishis. Some have wanted to do away with these medicines by substituting an invasion of new discoveries; however, humanity will again return to the foundations.

Here is a photograph of a man who walks through fire without harming himself. This is not fiction: witnesses will tell you of the same trials by fire in Madras, Lucknow, Benares. And not only does the Sadhu walk unharmed on the flaming coals, but he leads behind him those who desire to follow and hold on to him.

In Benares a Sadhu sits in sacred posture upon the water of the Ganges. His crossed legs are just below the surface of the water. The people flock to the banks, amazed at the holy man.

Still another Sadhu has been buried alive for many days; another swallow various poisons without any harm. Here is a Lama who can levitate himself; another Lama, by means of tumo, can generate his own heat, thus protecting himself against the snow and mountain glaciers; there a Lama can give the death stroke with his "deadly eye" to a mad dog. A venerated Lama from Bhutan relates how, during his stay at the Tzang district in Tibet, a Lama asked a ferryman to take him across from Tzampo free of charge; the clever man replied, "I will gladly take you over if you can prove that you are a great Lama. A mad dog is running about here doing great harm—kill it!" The Lama said nothing, but looking at the dog, he raised his hand and said a few words and the dog fell dead! The Bhutanese Lama saw this himself. One hears frequently in Tibet and India of the "deadly eye" and the "eye of Kapila." And on a 17th century map printed in Antwerp by authority of the Catholic clergy, the country of Shambhala is named!

If one can walk through fire, and another sit on water, a third remain suspended in air, a fourth repose on nails, a fifth swallow poison, sixth kill with a glance and a seventh lie buried without harm, then one may collect all those grains of knowledge in oneself. And thus the obstacles of lower matter can be transmuted! Not in a remote age, but now, right here where Millikan's cosmic rays, Rhine's thought transference and the reality of psychic energy are being studied and affirmed.

Every Rishi pronounced in his own language the sacred pledge for the construction of a revived, refined and beautiful world!

For the sake of a single righteous being a whole City was saved. As beacons, lightning rods and citadels of Good stood the Rishis of various nations, of various creeds, of various ages... yet one in the spirit of salvation and ascension for all!

Whether the Rishi arrived upon fire, upon a stone, upon the whirlwind—he always hastened for the general Good. Whether he prayed on a mountain summits, on a steep riverbank or in a hidden cave, he always sent out prayers for the unknown, for the stranger, for the laborers, for the sick and the crippled.

Whether the Rishi sent out white horses to save the unknown pilgrims or whether he blessed unknown seafarers or guarded a city by night, he always stood as a pillar of light for all, without extinguishing the flame.

Without condemnation, without mutual suspicion,

without weakening one another, ever upwards the Rishis ascended the eternal Mount Meru.

Before us is the road to Kailas. There rises one of the fifteen wonders described in Tibetan books: The Mount of the Bell! Along sharp ridges one climbs to its summit. It stands higher than the last junipers, higher than the last yellow and white mountain ranges. There Padma Sambhava once walked—this is recorded in the ancient monastery Gando-La. It is exactly here that the Caves of Milaraspa are situated. And not one by many has been sanctified with the name of the hermit, who hearkened before dawn to the voices of the Devas. Here also are the spiritual strongholds of Gautama Rishi. Not far away are also legends which surround Pahari Baba. Many Rishis walked here. And he who gave the mountain its enticing name "Mount of the Bell" also thought of the call of the Bell for all, of helping all, of the Universal Good!

Here Rishis live for Universal Good!

When Rishis meet on the mountain paths they do not ask each other: "From where do you come?" Is it from the East, or West, or South, or North? This is quite apparent: they come from Good and go to the Good. An exalted, refined, flaming heart knows where the Good is, and wherein it can be found.

Some of the travelers in our caravan were once discussing the qualities of the various Rishis. But a gray-haired pilgrim, pointing to the snowy peaks radiant in their consummate beauty said:

"Are we to judge the qualities of these Summits? We can but bow in admiration before their incomparable splendor!"

"Satyam, Shivam, Sundaram."

ASCENDING THE HEIGHTS

MANY expeditions are striving to conquer the magnificent peaks of the Himalayas. Severely the unconquered giants meet the daring intruders. Again, Everest refused to welcome newcomers. And Nanga Parbat does not help matters in the attempted conquest. And the Kanchenjunga peak is not even contested. Yet from all sides the various nations aspire to reach the resplendent Himalayan summits. Such a procession becomes the homage of pilgrims to the highest of the world.

The local lamas smile mysteriously when they hear that yet another attempt has been defeated. If they have confidence in you they will tell you in whispers some ancient prophecies which assert that certain sacred summits will never be defiled. Not long ago a well-known Lama, who is now dead, told us: "Curious people are the pelings: why do they undertake such dangers in the physical body, when we can visit these summits in our subtle body?"

Indeed, in every striving to the summits, in every ascent, is contained an untold joy. An inner impulse irresistibly calls people toward the heights.

If someone would begin to historically trace these aspirations which have the Himalayas as their goal, an unusually significant study would result. Truly, if one could trace the force of attraction to these heights for a thousand years, one could readily see why the Himalayas have been called "Incomparable." Since time immemorial have innumerable tokens of Divinity been connected with this country of mountains. Even in the dark middle ages, remote countries dreamed of beautiful India, which was epitomized in these mysterious, sacred, snowy giants. "Himalaya" means, in Sanskrit, "Abode of Snow."

Let us compare all these beautiful legends, which could only be conceived in the Himalayas. First of all, we would be astonished at the amazing diversity of this heritage. It is true that this wealth of legends has accumulated with many tribes, becoming more bounteous through the contribution of several millennia, and crowned by the achievements of great seekers of truth. All this is so. But for such supreme achievements, a magnificent environment is necessary.... and what could be more majestic than these unconquerable mountains with all their inexpressible radiance and exquisite variation of forms?

It would be a rather unfortunate and feeble effort to compare the Himalayas with any of the other splendid mountain ranges of the world. The Andes, the Caucasus, the Alps, the Altai—all the most beautiful heights will appear to be but single peaks when compared with the supreme mountain ranges of the Himalayas.

What does it not encompass, this multiform beauty? Tropical approaches, alpine slopes and finally, the innumerable glaciers powdered with meteoric dust. No one describes the Himalayas as overwhelming; no one would dare call them gloomy portals, or mention the word monotony in thinking of them. Truly, a great part of the human vocabulary must be forgotten when you enter the realm of the Himalayan snow—that part of one's vocabulary which is sinister or ineffectual.

The human spirit, seeking to overcome all obstacles, is filled with a yearning which irresistibly impels one toward the conquest of these summits. And the very difficulties which at times loom so dangerously become the most needed and desired steps of ascent, overcoming earthly conventionality. All the dangerous bamboo bridges over the thundering mountain torrents; all the slippery steps on the ages-old glaciers over perilous precipices; all the unavoidable inclines before each successive ascent; all the storms, thunder, cold and heat are surmounted, when the chalice of achievement is full.

The feelings of ambition or pride alone could not inspire so many travelers and seekers to go to the Himalayas. Other difficult peaks could be found for competition and contests. But above all thoughts of competition is a yearning toward these world-magnets, an ineffable holy aspiration of which heroes are born.

The true magnets are not the laurels of contests or the fleeting front pages of newspapers and magazines, but the attraction to this surpassing grandeur which sustains the spirit; and in such striving there can be no harm.

Why does one think of the Himalayas, why are we seemingly so compelled to remember them and strive toward them?

Because even mental communion with their solemn grandeur provides one of the best of tonics. Everything is impelled toward the beautiful in its own way. Everyone thinks about beauty and feels an impulse to express it in some way. The thought of beauty is so powerful and moving that man cannot contain it silently within himself, but always tries to clothe it in words. Perhaps in song, or in other expression of his being, man must manifest and record his thoughts of the beautiful.

From the tiniest flower, to the wing of the butterfly, to the glow of a crystal and onward, further and higher, through beautiful human forms, through mysterious sublime touch, man wants to fortify himself with the immutably Beautiful. Wherever on earth there have been creations by human hands, the pilgrim comes to them. He finds calm under their created vaults and in the radiance of their frescoes and stained glass. And if the pilgrim is captivated by mirages of nature's far off horizons, he will set out toward them. And if, at last, he becomes aware of these loftiest peaks shining far off, he is drawn to them and in this very striving becomes stronger, purer and inspired to achievements for the good, for beauty, and for ascent.

The pilgrim is always listened to with special attention

near the campfire or at a gathering of people. And not only in ancient chronicles does one read of the respect accorded to those who came from afar. Even now, despite all the speedy means of communication, when the world has become small, when people strive into the higher strata or down toward the center of the planet...even now, the narrative of the pilgrim still remains the highlight of every gathering.

"Are the Himalayas truly so beautiful?"

"Are they really incomparable?"

"Tell us something about the Himalayas and whether anything unusual is to be found there!"

People expect something unusual in every narrative of the pilgrim. Bad habits, old customs, immobility due to attachments, all these depress even the coarsest heart. Even a depressed spirit strives toward movement. After all, no one thinks of movement as only directed downward.

I recall the story that a traveler once related. Having begun the descent of the Grand Canyon in Arizona, surrounded by the most beautiful colors, he was yet oppressed by the very thought of such endless descent: "We descended lower and lower.... and even the thought of descending prevented our admiring the country."

Exaltation and transport are primarily connected with ascent. During ascent there is the urgent desire to look beyond the snowy peaks that soar before you. But when you descend, each parting summit pronounces a sad "goodbye." Therefore, it is joyous not only to ascend a summit, but to ascend in thought as well. When we hear of new travelers to the Himalayas we are thankful even for that, for they remind us of the summits and the call of the ever-beautiful, the ever-essential.

HIMALAYAN SONG

A Ladakhi Song:

THOUGH the gates of the East entered the Hindu
Faith.
Say, did you pass by the way of the sacred word?
The Persian kingdom erects the gates of the South.
Did you pass through them?
The celestial message of China opens to us the western
gates.
How did you pass the way of the Chinese Sign?
And the gates of the north belong to Gessar Khan.
How did you pass by the way of the sword stroke?
Did you pass the gates leading to Lhasa, where lies the
way of the seekers of truth?
The East—the gates of India. There, hallowing the
sacred word and custom, we rested.
The Persian kingdom possesses the gates of the south.
There we revered the border of the noble ones.
The celestial message of China opened to us the west-
ern gates.
Affirming the dates it gave us happiness.
The gates to the warrior, Gessar, are on the north.
By the clash of swords we passed these nations.
And through the gates of Lhasa, seeking for truth
We passed, testing in silence our spirit.

*(The geographical oddities of the song express the accumulations
of different races)*

Another beautiful Ladakhi song:

One is visited by wisdom and yet remains only
an onlooker.
Some can achieve wholly naught, therefore one must
test himself here.
But to him who already comes with wisdom, there is
special bliss.
Does the High One need the wisdom of nine signs?
And does the mediocre one need the same?
Are you coming as friend of high estate or do you
desire only a purse?
Do you come without threats?
Do you wish the covenant of friendship?
There are three kinds of enemies.
There are three kinds of friends.
Would you enumerate them?
An enemy who induces sickness.
An enemy who hates the spirit.
An enemy who avenges in bloodshed.
We did not come as enemies.
We are friend to you.
We name three friends:
Our Liberator Buddha,
The union of a harmonious family,
The union of love and blood.
Here are the three friends.
Verily, it is so.

FROM KAILAS

IN joy, in simplicity and in the unexpected, many revelations resound. And by no other term than revelation can these sparks of knowledge be called.

From Tibet comes a Lama. By appearance he is a simple pilgrim. His clothes are worn down to rags from his distant pilgrimage over the mountains and he has become weak, thin and burned bronze from heat and cold. He came to the Himalayas shortly before our departure. He was asked what visions he had or what remarkable dreams. At first he denied: "No, I have none; I am a simple Lama." A real Lama will never speak of his powers. He was asked again: "Should you see something, tell us." And the next morning the guest from the mountains came again and in a most quiet and simple voice he said: "I have seen." And in the same simple manner he described our entire planned journey, which could not have been known to any of the local inhabitants.

The journey was of course narrated figuratively, without names. But his descriptions surprised us by their accuracy and character. The trip by sea and the stay in Paris; then the tempest of the ocean; then America with its peculiarities, where there is so much movement, fiery energy and so many tall buildings. Then again, the ocean, snow and a country with many temples and tame animals. Then followed distinct hints at the Hingan hills, at many people good and bad. Then followed a description of another country with temples and a large image of Buddha, and then a country where people live in tents and yurtas, where there are many sheep and horses. These general descriptions were followed by a number of details, abounding with descriptive comparisons and gestures.

All of this was narrated in a quiet and simple way, as if the pilgrim were telling of his own travels. Likewise, he told the results of our trip, which could not be known by anyone. In all these cases of clairvoyance, one is especially astonished at the notable simplicity and directness—as if you were sitting in the recesses of a room, and someone approaching the window began telling you what was taking place in the street.

And was it not with the same remarkable simplicity that one of our companions was told eight months ago of his departure? The same date was repeated in words, quickly uttered. I also remember how, before the departure of the train, a nearby gypsy hastily told the departing lady a correct and important indication. I do not intend to repeat a great many cases of such foresight having taken place in the East, as well as many in the West, to which I was a witness. Much has been written about it and everyone knows that along with deliberate invention there exists a whole world of wonderful reality.

I would especially like to point out that the truest manifestations are always connected with an unusual simplicity and directness, and are very often impulsive in nature. Thus, often a man who has seen something speaks not when asked, but at times without even having been asked. And then, what is being said—even if very urgent—will be communicated quietly, quickly and almost indistinctly, as if it was supposed that someone may be attentively watching, and that he, whom this news concerns, is expecting it and will know how to accept it. Suddenness seems to correspond to vigilance. When in clear accord, people can understand each other with half a word. Likewise with clairvoyance: some sort of invisible string will resonate and call attention. Blessed are those who know how to preserve careful vigilance, which calls for preparedness. But true readiness is not formed by some forced concentration, but precisely by that simplicity which lies at the foundation of all significant actions and events.

One often hears about the correctness of first impressions and of the falseness of the subsequent ones. Unquestionably, the very first impressions come from the straight-knowledge of the heart and all the later impressions will be darkened by conventional reasoning. This is so. But how to distinguish the dividing line of the first impression from the subsequent ones?

Very often you can hear that a person complains of the inaccuracy of the first impression; but actually he has in mind not the first, but the second and perhaps even the third impression. For the sparks of enlightenment shine forth outside of time. Within living space, new combinations incessantly follow each other. Only the simplicity of a pure heart will faultlessly grasp the first sign and the first call. Such a heart will feel the sting of a lie and the coldness of concealed malice.

Therefore it is so joyful for all-embracing hearts to meet to exchange both verbal and silent talk, and to respond mutually, even at a distance. And the simpler, straighter and more direct these contacts of the hearts' currents are, the greater will be the mutual understanding and usefulness which result. Light, hardly audible are the touches of the wings of truth—they are sent down for the good, for true benefit. Only malicious accumulations lead the doubting travelers astray, into the wilderness and the abyss.

In time past, people addressed each other with the significant greeting, "Rejoice!" In this command of joy was also contained a wish for the purification of the heart for a better comprehension. In the pure air of the morning, in a joyful pure heart, great realizations are possible which are lost in the fusion of the sunset.

Too much of the low and earthly covers the heart, burdening and intoxicating it. Not in vain has it been repeated that the morning is wiser than the evening. Will not the expressions of true wisdom be the high and instantaneous realization of truth? And every such realization brings a wise joy—one which always preserves the quality of simplicity. Joy does not originate from complexity and contradictions. Joy lies within itself and has first and foremost the quality of directness and straightforwardness, and a smile for all things. It is joy which forms the bridge over all hostile obstacles. Joy is one of the best means for overcoming hostile attacks, and is of course, always the shortest path to exaltation.

The old greeting, "Rejoice!", even in those fragmentary records that have reached us, may have become conventional and lost its meaning. Nevertheless, the command of joy can be useful, even with a sad message. In this will be contained the wisdom of Solomon's message, which affirmed: "This, too, shall pass." He who could understand that short phrase "and this, too" to mean that many things accumulate and interchange, had to also understand the intricacies of life.

In the changing, fleeting reflections, the sparks of enlightenment are especially precious, when the distracted human consciousness can catch them. In the simplicity of straight-knowledge, faraway calls are received, more accurate and faster than any radio waves.

The Lama hurries.
"Why are you hurrying?"
"The Teacher calls; he is very ill, I must hasten."
"And where is thy Teacher?"
"In a cave in Kailas."
"But when did you receive the news? Kailas is many hundred miles away!"
"I received it this instant!"

Thus, words of great significance are pronounced with simplicity. At that moment, it was not important that news had been received which was confirmed months later, but it was important that one must hasten. Something quite common has taken place, something that is possible every day, which in simplicity is known as the call of straight-knowledge. The same simple straight-knowledge will whisper once more the significant "Rejoice!"—the command that leads out of the twilight—"Rejoice!"

URUSVATI

LAMA M. has started on visits to monasteries. Undoubtedly, he will again collect much significant information about both old traditions and medicinal matters. It is very good that he goes, for in this mobility is contained precisely that quality which I always recommend to our co-workers. The Tibetan physician D.T. also departs into the mountains. If he does not renew his supplies, if he puts off meeting with other doctor-Lamas, his store will soon be impoverished. Also two other co-workers are setting forth—one into Lahore, the other beyond the ocean.

When we founded the Institute, we had foremost in mind continuous mobility of labor. From the time of its foundation, there have been yearly expeditions and excursions. It would not be well to depart from this established tradition. If all the co-workers and correspondents were bound together in one place, how many excellent, yet unexpected, possibilities would be denied to them! And of course, people do not gather here, seated in one room, just to feed themselves with information sent to them. This would only be a halfway form of labor.

What is needed is that which the Hindus so heartily and significantly call the "ashram." This is the central point. But an ashram is nourished from many sources. Entirely unexpected wayfarers come to it, each bringing his own experience. Likewise, the co-workers of the "ashram" do not sit idle, but at every opportunity, go in different directions and augment their scientific supplies. Not without reason was it told long ago that a prior of a monastery said when the brethren went abroad: "Again our monastery is being broadened." It may have seemed that the brethren were scattering, but the prior actually considered this an extension of the monastery. And so, at present, every exchange of scientific forces, all expeditions and journeys, become an indispensable condition of progress. In this, people learn, and extend the limits of their own specialty. The traveler sees much. The wayfarer, if he is not blind, is able to perceive much that is remarkable. In the same manner, the narrowness of perception which once had such a hold upon humanity, is being replaced by a broad cognition.

It often happens that domains far removed from each other become beneficial co-workers. And it must be thus because the ultimate strivings of humanity, based upon collaboration, upon cooperation, must first of all learn synthesis. Still, not so long ago, people feared this unifying concept. Let us recall how Anatole France and many other enlightened writers were subtly ironical about specialization. Actually, in nature, all cooperates: everything is so blended and balanced that the conscious collaboration of people just responds to these basic laws of all that exists.

The usefulness of travel for the purpose of discerning the unlimited variety of all that exists has probably never before so occupied the minds of people as at present. The earthly globe will be quickly criss-crossed with traveled paths. Nevertheless, this will be only an early realization; on each of the paths, it will be necessary to both gaze loftily upwards and to penetrate deeply within, in order to appreciate the multiformity of possibilities which earlier, went unnoticed.

One thing is dangerous: in all this traveling, too many sporting trips and contests are being developed. In these purely external and mechanical competitions much is lost which is needed in our day. All contests of strength, endurance and speed must be replaced by contests of quickness and depth of thinking, of discernment.

Everyone has a store of anecdotes about classroom oddities and misunderstandings, and we need not repeat them, but let us very steadfastly remember that a one-sided technical education is not the goal.

No, all limited, conventional, technical schools are rendered archaic by the compelling concept of synthesis. If the technical school relies on the robot, the deeply-comprehended synthesis offers a new breadth of horizon. In the founding of branches of our establishments in different countries, we had precisely in mind that some time and somehow, the closest communication of co-workers would result. They enrich one another, they encourage one another, and they exchange the most useful concepts with one another. If then the establishments manifest the possibility for new cognitions, expeditions and visits, then let this possibility not be thrown aside.

Let us continue the already-formed tradition of mutual acquaintances. Let us look upon each new visit by our co-workers as a true development of instructive work. Yet for this, let us first develop true mobility.

When we speak about mobility, let us remember that it is not for the many. Many people like to talk about mobility. Seated in easy chairs at the evening table, they are ready to dream, to rise up and depart, to create and labor in new places. But as soon as it comes to carrying out these musings, many will find ten reasons which prevent them. Each of us can call to mind, even in the recent past, instructive episodes about those entirely prepared to set out on a distant path feebly sink back, detained in their easy chair. The reasons for the retreat were of course numerous, and deemed worthy of vital consideration!

When someone wishes to excuse himself for not doing something, you may be sure that he will find a great number of justifying causes. Thus, immobility will be praised by many; and yet mobility—that is, desire of new work, of new cognition—will be very easily censured. People will speak about empty dreaming, about unrealizable aspirations, about gullibility; few fail to show a resourceful ingenuity when they wish to avoid something whispered by the heart.

How many times have we read letters, full of aspiration at a distance, full of readiness for renewed work; but as soon as you ask the writer when he can set out on his new venture, he falls into a strange silence. Obviously, all the dustiness of life has beset the tongue of the heart and reduced it to silence. All the horned doubts have crawled forth, all the absurd considerations have been listened to, and still another possibility has been lost. It is not only that it has been lost to the individual, but that it could oppress and injure a great number of people near and far.

For the sake of imagined help to a few, cooperation and assistance in the great matters have been forgotten. The basic cause, however, is immobility, attachment to one's easy chair. And too, beyond immobility rises up the specter of fear for change in general. This specter leads to decay and senility. When such dissolution encroaches, it cannot be helped by external means. Yet often, some worthless thing has made people immobile. We ourselves have seen absolutely deplorable instances when people, apparently intelligent, have doomed themselves to the saddest sort of existence due to attachment to things. Ah, these things again! These rough tags of a dusty way of life. Sometimes they begin to rule to such an extent that the voice of the heart sounds not only improbable, but even irrelevant.

I always rejoice when I see mobility in co-workers.

LEGENDS

"WHEN the blue sky came into being and below it came the dark earth, then appeared between them man." Thus speaks an inscription of the eighth century, found on a stone near the river Orchon.

One feels in the brevity of this hieroglyph that the virgin steppes are not as yet tilled. The virgin taiga has not yet been desecrated. The depths of the earth are intact. And in these untouched vastnesses of a broad imagination, the great Mongolian, Kurultai, in the year 1206, proclaimed Ghengis Khan as the Emperor of the Universe.

This was possible.... as natural as the flight of an eagle of the steppes. Just as natural were the messages of Prester John to the rulers of Europe. These writings, until now, have been preserved in archives, but are now being diligently studied by researchers. It sounds like a fairy tale, yet at the same time the heart resounds to the past. The personality of Prester John was ascribed to many people and the description of his fairy tale-like country. At times it seems all is but a legend, but again, on a shelf in the archives the messages are preserved, the documents of embassies are safeguarded, and somewhere, the beautiful page of life is recorded.

Very likely, the true personality of Prester John will never be known—this leader of a great country who carried on negotiations with the rulers of the world. It does not matter how someone may solve this historic problem. One thing remains certain: something beautiful occupied many minds, and its very subtlety beckoned the possibility of new developments.

Note that while the saga of Gessar Khan, the way to

Shambhala and the kingdom of Prester John remained within the realm of legend, at the same time, certain searching scientists listened to these elusive calls of antiquity. And again, someone, feeling exalted by them, exclaimed: "What joy! What life! What boundlessness!"

An elderly woman healer tells a youth about ancient medical compounds, Silvery laughter and jokes interrupt her serious talk. But the experience of ages has taught the healer calmness: "Laugh, laugh! But go and ask all those whom my herbs have helped." From his early youth, Saint Panteleimon commands recognition as a healer. The Ayurvedic physician bends down over useful and good flowers and herbs. Every blade of grass of the steppes is full of ancient lore. Is this a fairy tale? How can it be a fairy tale when everything is full of great benefit?

Likewise, the beautiful voices of antiquity build the great saga of life, and a valiant Galahad, not afraid of fieriness, gathers sparks of fire into a design of Eternity. The searcher is not discouraged that, instead of kingly cities, before him lies only a hilly field. For in every hillock there may be a casket with some message of Prester John or a ring of Ghengis Khan. When everything seems to have been read in this world, from the depths of the earth appear complete, new, still-unread writings. From Harappa in India the attention of the scientists is directed to the Easter Islands in a seemingly futile search; such unusual actions begin to correspond to as-yet undeciphered riddles.

Life today, overtaxed and overburdened, responds to the simple hieroglyph if the imagination is vivid. What vigilance, what subtlety of thinking, when it is alive with the searches for Truth!

In great Rome, the stone head of the Statue of Trust bit the hands of liars. Truth does not tolerate falsehood. The heart knows wherein falsehood lies. The Heart is the Gate of Truth!

Mr. F.S. Smythe in his book *Camp Six* (1937), an account of the 1933 Mount Everest Expedition, says on page 105: ".... chancing to glance upwards my attention was caught by a tiny silvery object in the sky, apparently very high, moving rapidly from west to east. A second or two later it disappeared behind a shoulder of the range running southwards to the North peak. Was it an aeroplane? If so, it must be a machine of the Houston Everest Flight. But this was impossible; the last mail had brought us news of their successful flight over the mountain. Was it a bird? But what bird could gleam so brightly?

In Heart of Asia (1928), in the chapter "Shambhala" we read: "A sunny, unclouded morning—the blue sky is brilliant. Over our camp flies a huge, dark vulture. We and our Mongols watch it. Suddenly one of the Buryat Lamas points into the blue sky: "What is that? A white balloon? An aeroplane?" We notice something shiny, flying very high from the northeast to the south. We bring three powerful field glasses from the tents and watch the huge spheroid body shining against the sun, clearly visible against the blue sky and moving very fast. Afterwards we see that it sharply changes its direction from south to southwest and disappears behind the snow-peaked Humboldt Chain. The whole camp follows the unusual apparition and the Lamas whisper: "The Sign of Shambhala."

Travelers who came from Khotan have related that in 1927 they saw a bright object moving in the sky over the Kunlun range that they regarded as an aeroplane, but at that time, none could have been there. One could mention a similar event witnessed in Ladakhi by a botanical collector. Perhaps other similar testimonials could be gathered. One continually comes across many Himalayan phenomena in the press.

One could mention about a similar fact witnessed in Ladakh by a botanical collector. Perhaps other similar testimonials could be gathered. Continuously one comes across in the press of many Himalayan phenomena. Thus, in the same book (Heart of Asia) another most interesting occurrence is mentioned:

"In Nimu, a small village before Leh, we had an experience at eleven thousand feet which can under no circumstances be overlooked. It would be most interesting to hear of analogous cases. It was after a clear, calm day. We camped in tents. At about 10 pm I was already asleep when Mrs. Roerich approached her bed to remove the woolen rug. But hardly had she touched the wool when a big rose-violet flame, the color of an intense electric discharge, shot up, forming a seemingly whole bonfire, about a foot high. A shout of Mrs. Roerich, "Fire! Fire!" awoke me. Jumping up, I saw the dark silhouette of Mrs. Roerich and in front of her, a moving flame clearly illuminating the tent. Mrs. Roerich tried to extinguish the flame with her hands, but it flashed through her fingers and burst into several smaller fires. The effect to the touch was slightly warming, but there was no burning, no sound or odor. Gradually the flames diminished and finally disappeared, leaving no trace whatsoever on the bed cover. We had occasion to study many electric phenomena, but I must say that we never experienced one of such proportions."

Repeatedly, in descriptions of Himalayan travelers, one reads of the Himalayan glimmer and the Himalayan lights, something similar to the aurora borealis. Perhaps light could be shed on these phenomena by additional experiences. Such a colossal mountain region as the Himalayas indeed embraces many wonders.

IN HIS NAME

IN the temple, gigantic trumpets are sounding. The Lama asks: "Do you know why the trumpets of our temples have so resonant a tone?"

And he explains: "The rule of Tibet decided to summon from India—where the Blessed One dwelt—a learned Lama in order to purify the fundamentals of the teaching. How to meet the guest? The High Lama of Tibet, having a vision, gave the design of a new trumpet so that the guest should be received with an unprecedented sound; and the meeting was a wonderful one—not wrought by the wealth of gold, but by the grandeur of sound!

"And do you know why the gongs in the temple ring out with such great volume, and as silver resound the gongs and bells at dawn and evening, when the high currents are tense? Their sound reminds one of the beautiful legend of a Chinese emperor and a great Lama. In order to test the knowledge and clairvoyance of the Lama, the emperor made a seat from sacred books covered with fabrics for him and invited the guest to sit down. The Lama made certain prayers and then sat down. The emperor demanded of him, "If your knowledge is so universal, how could you sit down on the sacred books?" "There are no sacred volumes", answered the Lama. And the astonished emperor found only empty paper instead of his sacred volumes. The emperor thereupon gave many gifts and bells of liquid chine to the Lama, but the Lama ordered them to be thrown into the river, saying "I will not be able to carry these. If they are needed, the river will bring these gifts to me at my monastery." And indeed, the water carried the bells, with their crystal chines, clear as the waters of the river, to him."

And about talismans the Lama also explains:

"Sacred are held the talismans. A mother many times asked her son to bring to her a sacred relic of Buddha, but the youth forgot her request. She said. "Here will I die before your eyes, if you do not bring it to me now." The son went to Lhasa and again forgot the mother's request. A half day's journey from his house he called the promise, but where to find the sacred object in the desert? There is naught. But the traveler spied the skull of a dog. He decided to remove a tooth, and wrapping it in yellow silk, brought it to the house. The old woman asked of him, "Have you forgotten my last request, my son?" He then gave her the dog's tooth wrapped in silk, saying, "This is the tooth of Buddha." The mother put the tooth in her shrine, and performed before it the most sacred rites, directing all her worship to her Holy of Holies. And the miracle was accomplished: the tooth began to glow with a pure ray and many miracles occurred from it."

The neighborhood of Kuchar is full of ancient Buddhist cave temples, which gave so many beautiful monuments of Central Asiatic art. This art has, in full justice, received a high place among the monuments of ancient cultures. But despite the attention given to this art, it still seems to me that it has not yet been fully appreciated from the point of view of artistic composition.

The place of the late cave monastery close to Kuchar makes an unforgettable impression. In a gorge, rows of different caves are situated like an amphitheater, all decorated with wall paintings and showing traces of many statues, which must either have been destroyed or removed. One can well imagine the solemnity of this place at the time when the kingdom of the Uigurs was in full flourish. The wall paintings have partially remained. One often has reason to resent the European explorers who removed whole pieces of architectural ensembles to museums. If separate objects, which have already lost their connection to any definite monument, are taken away, there would be little to blame. But is it not unjust, from the local point of view, to forcibly remove portions of a composition which is still intact? Would it not be a pity to break Tuankhang, the best kept of the monuments of Central Asia, into pieces? We do not cut up Italian frescoes. But this consideration also has its justification. The majority of the Buddhist monuments in Moslem lands have been, and still are exposed to iconoclastic fanaticism. Bonfires are created in the caves for the purpose of destroying images, and wherever the hand can reach the faces of images, these have been scratched with knives.

We have seen the evidence of such destruction. The labor of such distinguished scholars as Sir Aurel Stein, Pelliot, Le Coq and Oldenburg have safeguarded many of the monuments, which otherwise were in the greatest danger of being destroyed because of the carelessness of the late Chinese administration. The old Central Asiatic artists showed a highly developed decorative feeling and a wealth of iconographic detail in harmony with generous composition over large surfaces. You can well imagine how many impressions are accumulated when every day, new observations are made, and when the generosity of nature and ancient times send inexhaustible artistic material.

A learned Lama, pointing down the hilly slopes of the mountain, said: "Down there near the stream is a remarkable cave, but the descent is very difficult. In the cave Kandro Sampo, near a hot spring not far from Tashiding, dwelt Padma Sambhava himself. A certain giant, thinking to penetrate across to Tibet, attempted to build a passage into the Sacred Land. The Blessed Teacher rose up and growing great in height struck the bold venturer. Thus was the giant destroyed. And now in the cave is the image of Padma Sambhava and behind it is a stone. It is known that behind this door, the Teacher had hidden secret mysteries for the future. But the dates for their revelation have not yet come."

At dusk, a gelong told of the Lord Maitreya: "A man searched for twelve years for Maitreya Buddha. Nowhere did he find him, and becoming very angry, he rejected his faith. As he walked along his way, he beheld one who was sawing through an iron rod with a horse hair, repeating to himself: "If the whole of life will not be enough, yet will I saw this through." Confusion fell on the wanderer. "What do my twelve years mean," he said, "in the face of such persistence? I shall return to my search." Thereupon there appeared before the man the Maitreya Buddha Himself Who said: "Long have I already been with thee, but thou didst not see Me, and thou repulsed Me and spat upon Me. I shall make a test. Go to the bazaar. I shall be upon thy shoulder." The man went, aware that he carried the Maitreya. But the men around him shrank from him, closing their noses and eyes. "Wherefore do you shrink from me, people?" he asked. "What a fright you have on your shoulders—an ill-smelling dog full of boils," they replied. Again the people did not see the Maitreya Buddha, for each one beheld only what he deserved to see."

Between Maral Bashi and Kuchar, our servant Suleiman pointed at the mountain to the southeast and said: "There, behind that mountain, live holy men. They left the world in order to save humanity through wisdom. Many have tried to go into their land, but few have ever reached it. They know that one has to go behind that mountain. But as soon as they cross the ridge, they lose their way."

Karashakhr is not only a stronghold of the Karashakhr Kalmucks, but this city was the last abode of the Chalice of Buddha as it was mentioned in the historiographs. The Chalice of the Blessed One was brought here from Peshawar, and here it disappeared.

Purushapura, or Peshawar, for a long time, was the City of the Chalice of Buddha. After the death of the Teacher, the Chalice was brought to Peshawar and was the object of deep reverence for a long time. At the time of the Chinese traveler Fahien, about 400 BC, the Chalice was still at Peshawar, in a monastery especially built for it. It was a many colored vessel. The lines of the edges of the four chalices of which it consisted could be clearly seen.

At the time of another Chinese traveler, Huen-Tsang, about 630 A.D., the Chalice was no longer at Peshawar. It was in Persia, or already in Karashakhr.

The Chalice of Buddha was wonder-working and inexhaustible—a true Chalice of Life.

Jataka tells of the origin of the Chalice:

"Then from the four lands came four guardians of the world and offered chalices made of sapphire. But Buddha refused them. Again they offered four chalices made of stone (muggavanna) and He, full of compassion for the four genii, accepted the four chalices.

He placed one into the other and ordained: 'Let there be one!'

And the edges of the four chalices became visible only as lines. All chalices formed one.

The Buddha accepted food into the newly-made Chalice, and having partaken of the food he offered thanks."

Lalita Vistara, telling of the sacraments of the Chalice of Buddha, attributes to the Blessed One the following significant address to the Kings who brought the chalices:

"Pay respect by the Chalice to Buddha and thou shalt be in the Chalice as in a vessel of knowledge."

"If thou wilst offer the Chalice to our equals, thou wilst not be left, neither in memory nor by judgment."

"Who offers the Chalice of Buddha will not be forgotten, neither in memory nor by wisdom."

This Chalice—the Ark of Life, the Chalice of Salvation—must be discovered again soon.

Thus they know in the deserts.

MYSTERIES

ON the Karakorum Pass, at nineteen thousand five hundred feet, on this highway, the highest in the world, the groom Goorban began to question me.

"What is it that has been secreted in these heights? It must be that a great treasure has been hidden hereabouts, as the way to this place is surely arduous. Having traversed all the passes, one may chance upon a smooth vault. Something tinkles under the horses' hooves. It must be that here are great secrets, but we do not know the entry-way to them. When will there be writings in books that reveal what has been hidden away, and where?"

All around this majestic Karakorum Pass, the white peaks glistened dazzlingly. All round us without a break rose a most brilliant scintillation. On the path itself, as if for a reminder, lay a great quantity of whitened bones. Were not some of these wayfarers going for treasures? Indeed, countless caravans have crossed the Karakorum for riches.

Here I am reminded of another tradition concerning a treasure. In Italy, at Orvieto, they related a remarkable legend to me about hidden artistic treasures. The story concerned either Duccio himself or one of his contemporaries. It was told in a lofty style that goes so well with the mellifluous Italian language.

"Just as it is nowadays, in olden times, the best artists were not always understood. For the beclouded eye, it has been difficult to evaluate forms, especially lofty ones. People have demanded nothing but the observance of old rules, and beauty has not often been accessible to them. It thus happened with the great artist of whom we are speaking. His best pictures, instead of exaltingly touching the hearts of people, were subjected to condemnation and mockery. For a long time, the artist endured this unjust attitude toward himself.

"In divine ecstasy he continued to create many masterpieces. Once he depicted a marvelous Madonna, but the envious prevented the hanging of this image in its predestined place. And this happened not once or twice, but several times. When the viper begins to creep in, it invades both palace and hovel.

"But the artist, made wiser and knowing the madness of the crowd was not distressed. He said: 'It has been given the bird to sing, and to me has been given the power to glorify lofty forms. As long as the bird lives it fills God's world with song. And so while I am alive, I shall also glorify it. Since the envious and the ignorant put obstacles in the way of my works, I shall not lead the evil ones into worse bitterness of heart. I shall collect the pictures rejected by them. I shall store them securely in oaken chests and, availing myself of the goodwill of my friend the abbot, I shall hide them in the deep cellars of the monastery. When the ordained day shall come, future generations will discover them. If, by the will of the Creator they must remain hidden, let it be so!'

"From this time on, people thought that the great artist had ceased painting. But hearing these suppositions, he only smiled, because henceforth he was not laboring for the sake of the people's joy, but for a higher beauty. And so, we do not know where this priceless treasure is preserved."

"No one knows in precisely what monastery, in what secret vaults, the artist concealed his creations. True, in certain cloisters, old paintings have been found in crypts, but these have been found singly; they were not purposefully deposited there, and therefore could not be the treasure intentionally hidden by the great artist. Indeed in the underground vaults they continue to sing 'Gloria in Excelsis', but searchers have not been fortunate enough to find what was indicated by the artist himself. Certainly we have many monasteries and still more temples and castles that lie in ruins. Who knows, perhaps the tradition relates to one of these remains, already destroyed and razed by time.

"But have you been assured that this treasure is hidden within the boundaries of Italy?" asked one of the listeners.

"Of course even in remote times people were going to other countries. May it not be that these treasures have likewise been unexpectedly dispersed, or rather, preserved in different countries?" Another person added: "It may be that this story does not at all refer to a single master. Of course human practices are often repeated. Consequently, we find in history repetitions of human wanderings and ascents."

When we reached the middle of the Karakorum Pass, the groom Goorban said to me: "Give me a couple of rupees. I will bury them here. Let us too add to the great treasures."

I asked him: "Then do you think that treasures have been collected together there below? He looked surprised, even frightened. "But does the sahib not know? Even to us lowly people it is known that there, deep down, are extensive underground vaults. In them have been gathered treasures from the beginning of the world. There are also great guardians. Some have been fortunate enough to see how, from the hidden entry-ways, come tall white men, who then again withdraw underground. Sometimes they appear with torches, and many caravaneers know these fires. These subterranean beings do no evil. They even help people.

"I know, for a fact, that one local boy was lost from his caravan in a snowstorm and covered his head in despair. Then it seemed to him that someone was moving around him. He looked around in the darkness but there appeared no horse, no man—he saw nothing. Yet, when he put his hand in his pocket, he found a handful of gold pieces.

Thus do the great dwellers of the mountains help miserable people in misfortune."

And again the stories came to mind about the secret magnets established by the followers of the great philosopher and traveler, Apollonius of Tyana.

It is said that in definite places where it had been ordained that new states be built up or great cities erected, or that great discoveries and revelations should take place, there, on all such sites were implanted portions of a giant meteor, sent from the distant luminaries.

There has even been a custom of testifying to the truth of statements by reference to such ordained places. Deponents would say: "What I have said is as true as the fact that on a certain site has been placed such and such..."

The groom Goorban again raised the question: "Why do you foreigners who know so much not find the entryway into the underground kingdom? You know how to do everything and boast of knowing everything, and yet you do not enter into the secrets which are guarded by the great fire!"

"Man lives in mysteries,
and these are numberless!"

RISHIS

O N Himalayan slopes the Blessed Rishi Charaka collected healing herbs. Nature awaits here full of gifts.
Come hither and be cured. Charura, Parura, Orrura are
the three important curative fruits against cough, cold and
fever. Charura is like a yellow cherry, Parura like a green
chestnut, and Orrura like a yellowish-green crab-apple.
All three are sharp to the taste and full of tannin.

Here is the red bark of Aku Ombo, to cure wounds.
Salve against fever is Sergi Phurba, like a dry giant bean.

Chuta, the dry bitter root, will cure swelling and heal
the throat. Bassack is the brown powder for colds. The
red-stemmed Tze produces magenta; bitter Purma is for
incense. A broth from the roots of Berekuro is effective for
women's ailments. The flowers of Dangero heal the stom-
ach, much like the flowers of red rhododendron, while the
leaf of Dystro is a disinfectant for wounds.

Memshing Pati is a sacred plant in Nepal, where it
is used for ornaments at festivals. Endless are the useful
plants awaiting application and study.

The leaves of the herb Ava Duti are said "to soften"
stones, just as do the legendary "snow frogs"[1] of the Himalayas. Therefore if upon a stone you see the print of an
elk's foot or the paw of an animal, it seems they have
touched or eaten this wondrous herb.

Turning again to legends: near Phalut on the road to
Kanchenjunga grows a precious plant, the black aconite.
Its flower lights up at night, and by its glow, one locates
this rare plant. Here again is a reminder of the legend of

---

[1] A legend that attributes the ability to soften stones to "snow-frogs."

the Russian fire flower, the enchanted blossom that fulfills all wishes—and leads us not to superstition but to that same source wherein so much still lies concealed.

On this hillock, Rishi Sarakha has sent his benevolent arrow. On Rohtang, Rishi Vyasa has recorded the Mahabharata; on the glaciers, Rishi Khambhala gave his life as his last sacrifice for Humanity.

Unselfish Work, all for the Common Good.

HIMALAYAN PROPHECIES

PROPHECIES OF SHAMBHALA AND MAITREYA

THE Treasure is returning from the West. On the Mountains, the fires of jubilation are kindled.

There walk those who carry the Stone. Upon the Shrine are the signs of Maitreya. Out of the Secret Kingdom is given the date when the carpet of expectation may be spread. By the signs of the seven stars shall the Gates be opened.

By Fire shall I manifest My Messengers.

Gather the prophecies of your happiness.

* * *

Thus are the prophecies of the ancestors and the writing of the wise ones fulfilled. Gather thy understanding to hail the predestined.

When in the fifth Year, the heralds of the warriors of Northern Shambhala shall appear, gather understanding to meet them. And receive the New Glory! I shall manifest my sign of Lightning.

* * *

THE COMMAND OF GESSAR KHAN

I have many treasures, but only upon the appointed day may I bestow them upon My People. When the legions of Northern Shambhala shall bring the Spear of Salvation, then shall I unveil the depths of the mountain, and you will divide My Treasures equally among the warriors and yourselves and live in justice.

The time shall soon come for My command to cross all deserts. When my gold was scattered by the winds, I ordained the day when people of Northern Shambhala would come to gather My possessions. Then shall My people prepare their bags for the treasures. And to each shall I give a just share.

* * *

One may find sands of gold. One may find precious gems. But true wealth will come only with the People of Northern Shambhala when the time comes to send them forth.

Thus, it is ordained.

* * *

It is predicted that the manifestation of Maitreya shall come after the wars. But the final war shall be for the True Teaching, and each one rising up against Shambhala shall be stricken in all his deeds, and the waves shall wash away his dwellings.

And not even a dog shall answer his call. Not clouds, but lightning shall he see on the final night.

And the fiery messenger shall rise up on pillars of Light. The teaching indicates that each warrior of Shambhala shall be named the Invincible.

The Lord Himself hastens. His Banner is already above the mountains.

* * *

Thy pastures shall reach the Promised Land. When thou tendest thy flocks, doest thou not hear the voices of the stones? These are the toilers of Maitreya who make the treasures ready for thee.

When the wind murmurs through the reeds, dost thou understand that these are the arrows of Maitreya, flying in protection?

When the lightning illumines your camps, knowest that this is the light of the desired Maitreya?

To whom shall the watch upon the first night be entrusted?—to thee. To whom shall My Envoy be dispatched?—to thee. Who shall meet Him?—thou.

From the West, from the mountains shall My People come. Who shall receive and safeguard them?—thou.

Beseech the Tarn to rest with thee. Will to cleanse thy heart until My Coming.

Each one hearing My request shall cover his head with a fiery cover and shall entwine the head strap of his horse with a fiery cord.

Look carefully upon the rings of the coming ones. My Chalice is where there is thy salvation. Upon the mountains, fires are kindled.

Coming is the New Year. Who shall slumber through it shall not awaken again. Northern Shambhala has come!

We know not fear. We know not depression. Dukkar, the many-eyed and many-armed, sends us pure thoughts. Ponder with pure thoughts. Ponder with thoughts of light.

* * *

One-two-three! I see three peoples.

One-two-three! I see three books. The first is of the Blessed One Himself. The second is given by Ashvagosha. The third is given by Tzong-kha-pa.

One-two-three! I see three books of the coming of Maitreya. The first is written in the West. The second is written in the East. The third is written in the North.

One-two-three! I see three manifestations. The first is with the sword. The second is with the law. The third is with the light.

One-two-three! I see three horses. The first is black. The second is red. The third is white.

One-two-three! I see three ships. The first is on the waters. The second is under the waters. The third is above the earth.

One-two-three! I see three eagles. The first is perched upon the stone. The second is pecking his prey. The third is flying toward the sun.

One-two-three! I see the seekers of light. Red Ray! Blue Ray! Ray of silvery-white!

* * *

I affirm that the Teaching issued from Bodh Gaya shall return there. When the procession carrying the Image of Shambhala shall pass through the lands of Buddha and return to the first source, then the time of the pronunciation of the sacred word of Shambhala shall arrive.

Solemnly I affirm: Shambhala the invincible!

Then shall one receive honor from the pronouncement of this name. Then shall the thought of Shambhala provide sustenance. Then shall affirmation of Shambhala become the beginning of all works and gratitude to Shambhala their end. And both great and small shall be filled with understanding of the Teaching.

Sacred Shambhala is pictured amidst the swords and spears in impenetrable armor.

Fulfilled is the circle of the bearing of the Image! The Image is brought in the sites of Buddha and in those of Maitreya. "Kalagiya" is pronounced.

As the banner of the Image unfurls: What has been pronounced is as true as that under the Stone of Ghum lies the Prophecy of Sacred Shambhala.

The Banner of Shambhala shall encircle the central lands of the Blessed Ones. Those who accept Him shall rejoice. And those who deny Him shall tremble.

The Tashi Lama shall ask the Great Dalai Lama: "What is predestined for the last Dalai Lama?"

The Tashi Lama shall be given over to justice and shall be forgotten. And the warriors shall march under the Banner of Maitreya. And the city of Lhasa shall be obscured and deserted.

"Those rising up against Shambhala shall be cast down.

[60]

To the stricken ones, the Banner of Maitreya shall flow as blood over the lands of the new world; to those who have understood, as a red sun."

The Tashi Lama shall find the Great Dalai Lama and the Great Dalai Lama shall address him: "I will send thee the worthiest sign of my lightning. Go overtake Tibet. The ring shall protect thee."

* * *

Let us also remember some Hindu traditions.

The Kalki Purana mentions the Kalki Avatar that is yet to come:

"At your request, I shall take birth in the abode Shambhala. I shall again place the two rulers Maru and Devapi on earth. I shall create Satya-Yuga and restore the Dharma to its former condition, and after destroying the serpent Kali, I shall return to my own abode..."

Vishnu Purana continues:

"Devapi and Maru...living above Kalapa and endowed with great yogic powers will, together guided by Vasudeva, at the end of Kali, establish Varna and Ashrama Dharma as before."

Shirmad Bhagavata in Book VI says:

"These Maharshis and other great Siddhas are purposefully moving about on the face of the earth unnoticed in order to provide spiritual enlightenment to those, like Me, who follow worldly attractions."

Shankaracharya in his *Viveka Chudamani* says:

"Those Great Ones who have attained peace and who Themselves have finished swimming across the fearful ocean of births and deaths exist and move for the good of the people as does the Spring. They liberate mankind without selfish motive."

The *Vishnu Purana* speaks of the end of Kali-Yuga, when barbarians will be masters on the banks of the Indus:

"There will be contemporary monarchs reigning over the earth, kings of churlish spirit, violent temper and ever addicted to falsehood and wickedness. They will inflict death upon women and children, and they will seize upon the property of their subjects.... Their lives will be short, their desires insatiable.... People of various countries will intermingle with them.... Wealth will decrease, until the world will be wholly depraved.

"Property alone will confer rank; wealth will be the only source of devotion.... Passion will be the sole bond of union between the sexes. Falsehood will be the only means of success in litigation. Women will be objects merely of sensual gratification. A rich man will be reputed pure. Fine clothes will signal dignity....

"Thus in the Kali Age, decay will proceed upon decay.... At the close of the Kali-Yuga, the Kalki Avatar shall descend upon earth. He will reestablish righteousness...When the Sun and Moon and Tishya and the planet Jupiter are in one mansion, the Satya Age will return the White Age!"

The *Agni Purana* says the following:

"At the end of the Kali-Yuga, there will be mixed castes, and robbers without character will flourish. Under the cover of religion, they will preach irreligion. And the Mlechhas, in the guise of kings, will devour men. Armed with a coat of mail and weapons, Vishnuyasha's son Kalki will exterminate the Mlechhas, establish order and dignity, and lead the people on the path of truth. Then having renounced the form of Kalki Hari will return to heaven. Thereupon, Krita-Yuga will come into existence as before."

* * *

It is told in the prophecies how the New Era shall manifest itself: "First an unprecedented war of all nations will begin. Afterwards, brother shall rise against brother. Oceans of blood shall flow, and the people shall cease to understand one another. They shall forget the meaning of the word Teacher. But just then the Teacher shall appear and in all corners of the world, the true teaching shall be heard. The people shall be drawn to this word of truth, but those who are filled with darkness and ignorance shall raise obstacles.

"As a diamond glows the light on the Tower of the Lord of Shambhala. One Stone of His ring is worth more than all the world's treasure. Even those who by accident help the Teaching of Shambhala will receive in return a hundredfold.

"Already many warriors of the teachings of truth are incarnated. Only a few years shall elapse before every one shall hear the mighty steps of the Lord of the New Era. And one can already perceive unusual manifestations and encounter unusual people. Already they open the gates of knowledge and ripened fruits are falling from the trees."

SHAMBHALA

IF I should tell you the most sacred word of Asia—Shambhala—you will be silent. If I should tell you the same name in Sanskrit—Kalapa—you will be silent. If I should tell you the name of the mighty Ruler of Shambhala—Rigden-jyepo—even this mighty name of Asia will not move you. But it is not your fault. All indications about Shambhala are scattered throughout literature, and not one book has yet been written in any of the Western languages about this stronghold of Asia. But if you have in mind to be understood in Asia and approach her as a welcome guest, you must meet the host with the most sacred words and show that these conceptions are for you not mere empty sounds but that you value them and understand them with the highest meaning.

The Buryat scholar Baradin, in his latest book *Monasteries of Mongolia and Tibet*, states, amidst various other information that lately monasteries in honor of Shambhala have been founded in China and Mongolia, and in existing monasteries, special datsans of Shambhala—Shambhalin-Datsans have been instituted.

No doubt to the casual onlooker, this information may sound somehow metaphysical and abstract, or unnecessary. To the superficial observer, such news may appear as yet another grain of superstition and will certainly seem to be without reality, the world today being drowned in political and commercial speculation.

But the attentive observer, who has himself traversed the depths of Asia, will feel entirely differently. For him, this news will be full of reality, full of deep meaning for the future. In this short communication, the person in touch with Asia will feel again how alive are all the so-called prophecies and legends there which come from the most ancient sources. The oldest *Vedas*, the still older *Puranas* and a whole literature, varied in its sources, affirm the extraordinary meaning for Asia of the mysterious word Shambhala.

And in the large population centers, where sacred conceptions are already pronounced with a careful look around, and in the endless deserts of the Mongolian Gobi, this word of the Great Shambhala or the mysterious Kala-pa of the Hindus is the most real symbol of the great Future. In these words about Shambhala, in the narra-tives, legends, songs and folklore, is contained what is per-haps the most important message of the East. He who yet knows nothing of Shambhala has no right to state that he has studied the East and knows contemporary Asia.

Before starting to speak of Shambhala itself, let us remember the Messianic concepts, which are to be found in the most diverse nations of Asia and which, in their striving, unite a great variety of people into one great expectation of the future.

The Palestinic strivings toward a Messiah are well-known. Broad masses await a great incarnation near the border of the Bridge of the Worlds. People know the white horse, and the fiery sword like a comet, and the radi-ant appearance of the Great Rider above the skies. The learned rabbis and scholars of the Kabalah scattered all over Palestine, Syria and Iran will tell you many remark-able things on this subject.

The Moslems of Iran, Arabia, of Chinese Turkestan sacredly guard the legend of Muntazar, who in the near future will lay the foundation of the New Era. It is true that many mullahs, when you speak to them of Muntazar, will in the beginning sharply deny this, but if you contin-ue to insist with sufficient assertion and show a sufficient knowledge, they will smile vaguely and put away their negations, and they will often add many important details. And if you continue and tell them that in Isfahan the white horse that is destined to carry the Great Comer has already been saddled, the mullahs will look at each other and add that in Mecca, a Great Tomb has already been prepared for the Prophet of the Truth.

The most learned Japanese, the best scholars, can speak highly of the expected Avatar, and the learned Brahmins, taking their knowledge from the *Vishnu Purana* and the *Devi Purana*, will quote beautiful lines about the Kalki Avatar on the white horse.

For the moment, I shall not touch any inner signs now accumulated around the conception of Shambhala.

To give a more realistic impression, I first want to tell you simply how and where we came in touch with people who know and are already devoted to the Great Conception of Asia. Perhaps we already knew about Shambhala. We had read the translation by Professor Grünwedel of the Tibetan manuscript entitled *The Road to Shambhala*, written by the Third Tashi Lama, one of the most esteemed high priests of Tibet. Let us go through the wayside signs which met us during our travels.

In Ghum monastery, not far from the Nepalese frontier, you see in the temple a huge image of the Buddha-Maitreya, the next coming Savior and Ruler of Humanity, instead of the usual central figure of Buddha. This image is made like the great image of Maitreya in Tashi Lumpo, the seat of the Tashi Lama, spiritual ruler of Tibet, near Shigatse. The Lord Maitreya is seated on His throne, and His feet are not cross-legged as usual, but are positioned on the floor. This is a sign that the time of His Coming is near, and that the Ruler is already preparing to descend from His throne. This monastery was built about forty years ago by a learned Mongolian Lama who came from faraway Mongolia to Tibet and crossed the Himalayas to Sikkim, where the red sect of Padmasambhava represents the official religion. He came to erect this new monastery and to proclaim the approaching advent of the Lord Maitreya.

In 1924, a learned Lama, a faithful disciple of the

founder of this monastery who had received the profound Teaching and many prophecies for the future from him, told us in front of the impressive image: "Verily, the time of the great advent is nearing and according to our prophecies, the epoch of Shambhala has already begun. Rigden-jyepo, the Rule of Shambhala, is already preparing his unconquerable army for the last fight. All his assistants and officers are already incarnating.

"Have you seen the thanka-banner of the Rule of Shambhala for his fight against the evil forces? When our Tashi Lama had to flee from Tibet recently, he took with him only a few banners, but amongst them, several banners about Shambhala. Many learned Lamas fled from Tashi Lumpo and just now, a geshe (learned) painter, a gelong of Tashi Lumpo has arrived from Tibet. He knows how to paint the thanka of Shambhala. There are several variations of this subject, but you should have the one with the battle in the lower part of the painting in your home."

Shortly after this, Lariva, the artist Lama, was sitting on a rug in the white gallery of our home; he was outlining the complicated composition on the white surface of a specially prepared canvas. In the middle of it was the Mighty Ruler of Shambhala in the glory of His majestic abode. Below was the ferocious battle in which the enemies of the Righteous Ruler were unmercifully destroyed. As a dedication, the banner was adorned with this inscription: "To the Illustrious Rigden, King of Northern Shambhala."

It was touching to observe with what respect and veneration the artist lama worked. And when he pronounced the name of the Ruler of Shambhala, he put his hands together as in prayer.

Just at the time of our arrival in Sikkhim the Tashi Lama fled from Tashi Lumpo to China. Everybody was startled by this unprecedented action of the spiritual head of Tibet. The Lhasa government, in confusion, began searching everywhere; but rumors were already circulating that the Tashi Lama had passed through Calcutta in disguise.

Referring to this event a lama told us: "Verily the old prophecies are fulfilled. The time of Shambhala has come. For centuries and centuries it has been predicted that many wondrous events will occur before the time of Shambhala has come, many wonderful events will occur, but many ferocious wars will also devastate countries, many thrones will fall, many earthquakes will take place and Panchen Rimpoche will leave his abode in Tashi Lumpo in Tibet. Verily the time of Shambhala has come. The great war has devastated countries, many thrones have perished, earthquakes have destroyed old temples in Japan, and now our revered Ruler has left his country."

Following the spiritual ruler from Tibet, Geshe Rimpoche from Chumbi, one of the most esteemed high priests whom the Tibetans regard as an incarnation of Tzon-Kha-Pa, arrived. The high priest traveled through Sikkhim, India, Nepal and Ladak with several faithful lamas and lama artists, everywhere erecting images of the Blessed Maitreya and teaching about Shambhala.

When the high priest, with his numerous attendants visited Talai-Pho-Brang, our home in Darjeeling, he first of all paid attention to the image of Rigden-jyepo, the Ruler of Shambhala, and said:

"I see you know that Shambhala has approached. The nearest path for attainment is now only through Rigden-jyepo. If you know the Teaching of Shambhala, you know the future."

During his subsequent visits to us, the high priest spoke more than once of Kalachakra, not only giving an ecclesiastical meaning to this teaching, but applying it to life as a real Yoga. In 1927 of our era, one can, for the first time, meet the teaching of Kalachakra spread by Attisha. This is the high Yoga of using high powers hidden in the human body and connecting them with cosmic energies. From ancient times, special schools of Shambhala have been established only in a few monasteries—in the more learned ones. The chief place of the vital Yoga was always Tashi Lumpo, because Tashi Lamas have been high protectors of Kalachakra and were closely linked with Shambhala. In Lhasa, Moruling is considered one of the most learned monasteries practicing Kalachakra. In this monastery, there are only about three hundred Lamas. It is said that from time to time, the most learned of them go to a mysterious retreat in the Himalayas.

ABODE OF LIGHT

"LAMA, tell me of Shambhala!"

"But you Westerners know nothing about Shambhala—you wish to know nothing. You probably ask only out of curiosity, and you pronounce this sacred word in vain."

"Lama, I do not ask about Shambhala aimlessly. People everywhere know of this great symbol under different names. Our scientists seek each spark concerning this remarkable realm. Csoma de Koros knew of Shambhala when he made his prolonged visit to the Buddhist monasteries. Grünwedel translated the book of the famous Tashi Lama Pal-den-ye-she, *The Way to Shambhala*. We sense how, under secret symbols, a great truth is concealed. Truly, the ardent scientist desires to know all about Kalachakra."

"How can this be so, when some of your Western people desecrate our temples? They smoke within our holy sanctuaries; they neither understand nor wish to venerate our faith and our teaching. They mock and deride the symbols whose meaning they do not penetrate. Should we visit your temples, our conduct would be completely different because your great Bodhisattva, Issa, is verily an exalted one. And none of us would defame the teaching of mercy and righteousness."

Lama, only the very ignorant and stupid would ridicule your teaching, All the teachings of righteousness are as in one sacred place. And each one possessed of his senses will not violate the sacred place. Lama, why do you think that the essential teaching of the Blessed One is unknown to the West? Why do you believe that in the West we know nothing of Shambhala?

Lama, upon my very table you may see the Kalachakra, the Teaching brought by the great Attisha from India. I know that if a high spirit, already prepared, hears a voice proclaiming *Kalagiya*, it is the call to Shambhala. We know which Tashi Lama visited Shambhala. We know the book of the High Priest, T'aishan, *The Red Path to Shambhala*. We even know the Mongolian song about Shambhala. Who knows—perhaps we know many things. We know that quite recently a young Mongolian Lama issued a new book about Shambhala."

The Lama studies us with his piercing gaze. Then he says:

"Great Shambhala is far beyond the ocean. It is the mighty heavenly domain. It has nothing to do with our earth. How and why do you earthly people take such an interest in it? Only in some places, in the Far North, can you discern the resplendent rays of Shambhala."

"Lama, we know the greatness of Shambhala. We know the reality of this indescribable realm. But we also know about the reality of the earthly Shambhala. We know how some high lamas went to Shambhala, how along their way they saw the customary physical things. We know the stories of the Buryat lama, of how he was accompanied through a very narrow, secret passage. We know how another visitor saw a caravan of hill people with salt from the lakes on the very borders of Shambhala. Moreover, we ourselves have seen a white frontier post of one of the three outposts of Shambhala. So, do not speak to me about the heavenly Shambhala only, but also about the one on earth; do not speak to me about the heavenly Shambhala only, but also about the one on earth, because you know as well as I that the earthly Shambhala is connected with the heavenly one. And in this link the two worlds are unified."

The Lama became silent. With eyes half concealed by the lids, he examines our faces. And in the evening dusk he commences his tale: "Verily, the time is coming when the Teaching of the Blessed One will come once again from the North to the South. The word of Truth, which started its great path from Bodh Gaya, shall again return to the same sites. We must accept it simply, as it is: the fact that the true teaching shall leave Tibet, and shall appear again in the South. Really, great things are coming. You come from the West, yet you are bringing news of Shambhala. Verily, we must accept this. The ray from the tower of Rigden-jyepo has reached all countries.

"Like a diamond glows the light on the Tower of Shambhala. He is there—Rigden-jyepo, indefatigable, ever vigilant in the cause of mankind. His eyes never close. And in His magic mirror, He sees all events of earth. And the might of His thought penetrates into far-off lands. Distance does not exist for Him; He can instantaneously bring assistance to worthy ones. His powerful light can destroy all darkness. His immeasurable riches are ready to aid all needy ones who offer to serve the cause of righteousness. He may even change the karma of human beings..."

"Lama, it seems to me that you speak of Maitreya; is it not so?"

"We must not pronounce this mystery! There is much which may not be revealed. There is much which may not be crystallized into sound. In sound we reveal our thoughts. In sound we project our thought into space and the greatest harm may follow, because everything divulged before the destined date results in untold harm. Even the greatest catastrophes may be provoked by such light-minded acts. If Rigden-jyepo and the Blessed Maitreya are one and the same for you—let it be so. I have not so stated!

"Uncountable are the inhabitants of Shambhala. Numerous are the splendid new forces and achievements which are being prepared there for humanity...."

"Lama, Ancient Teachings tell us that very soon new energies shall be given to humanity. Is this true?"

"Innumerable are the great things predestined and prepared. Through the Holy Scriptures we know of the Teaching of the Blessed One about the inhabitants of the distant stars. From the same source we have heard of the flying steel bird.... about an iron serpent which devours space with fire and smoke. Tathagata, the Blessed One, predicted all for the future."

"Lama, if the great warriors are incarnated, will not the activities of Shambhala take place here on our earth?"

"Everywhere—here and in heaven. All benevolent forces shall come together to destroy the darkness. Each one who will help in this great task shall be rewarded a hundred fold, and upon this earth, in this incarnation. All sinners against Shambhala will perish in this very incarnation, because they have exhausted mercy."

"Lama, we certainly know that Panchen Rimpoche is greatly esteemed everywhere. In different countries we have heard how highly, not only Buddhists, but the people of many nations talk about His Holiness. It is even said that in his private apartments, long before his departure, the details of his coming travels were depicted in the frescoes. We know that Panchen Rimpoche follows the customs of all the great lamas. We have been told how during his flight, he and his followers escaped many of the greatest dangers.

"We know how at one time his pursuers from Lhasa were already quite upon him, when a heavy snowfall cut off the pursuers' road. Another day, Panchen Rimpoche arrived at a lake in the mountains; a difficult problem confronted him. His enemies were close behind, but in order to escape, it would be necessary for him to make a long circuit around the lake. Thereupon, Panchen Rimpoche sat in deep meditation for some time. Arousing himself, he gave orders that despite the danger, the entire caravan would have to spend the night on the shores of the lake. Then, the unusual happened. During the night, a heavy frost developed, which covered the lake with ice and snow. Before sunrise, while it was still dark, the Tashi Lama gave orders to his people to move on speedily; he, with his three hundred followers crossed the lake by the shortest way, thus escaping danger. When the enemies arrived at the same spot, the sun was already high and its rays had melted the ice. There remained for them only the round-about way. Was it not so?"

"Verily, so it was. Panchen Rimpoche was helped by Holy Shambhala throughout his travels. He saw many wondrous signs when he crossed the uplands while hastening to the North."

"Lama, not far from Ulan-Davan we saw a huge black vulture which flew low, close to our camp. He crossed the path of something shining and beautiful, which was flying south over our camp, and which glistened in the rays of the sun."

"The eyes of the Lama sparkled. Eagerly he asked:

"Did you also sense the perfumes of the temple-incenses in the desert?"

"Lama, you are quite right—in the stony desert, several days from any habitation, many of us became simultaneously aware of an exquisite breath of perfume. This happened several times. We never smelled such a lovely perfume. It reminded me of a certain incense which a friend of mine once gave me in India—from where he obtained it, I do not know."

"Ah—you are guarded by Shambhala. The huge black vulture is your enemy who is eager to destroy your work; but the protecting force from Shambhala follows you in this Radiant form of Matter. This force is always near you, but you cannot always perceive it. Sometimes, it is manifested only for strengthening and directing you. Did you notice the direction in which the sphere moved? You must follow the same direction. You mentioned to me the sacred call—*Kalagiya!* When someone hears this imperative call, he must know that the way to Shambhala is open to him. He must remember the year when he was called, because from that time evermore, he is closely assisted by the Blessed Rigden-jyepo. Only you must know and realize the manner in which people are helped, because often people repel the help which is sent."

KNOWLEDGE OF EXPERIENCE

"LAMA, tell me, how are the simple people helped by Shambhala? We know of Rishis and of incarnate co-workers of Shambhala, but in what manner does the might of Shambhala manifest itself among the humble?"

"In untold and manifold ways. Each one who in previous incarnations followed the teaching of righteousness and was useful to the Common Cause is helped by Shambhala. Not many years ago, during the war and unrest, one man asked a Lama if he should change his dwelling. The Lama answered that he could remain in the same place for about six months longer, but afterwards, he would be in great danger and would have to flee without delay. During the six months that followed, the man was most successful in his work; everything was peaceful and his possessions multiplied. When the six months expired, he thought: "Why should I risk my property by leaving this quiet spot? Everything seems so prosperous for me and there is apparently no danger. Probably the Lama was mistaken."

"But the danger suddenly arose. The enemy troops approached the place at full speed from both directions. And the man realized that his best opportunity had been lost and his way was now cut off. He hurried to the same Lama and told of what had happened.

"The Lama told him that for certain reasons it was necessary that he be saved. 'But,' he added, 'it is now more difficult to help you. The best opportunity is lost, but I can still do something for you. Tomorrow, take your family with you and ride towards the North. On the road you will meet your enemies. This is inevitable. When you see them coming, step off from the road and remain quiet. Even though they may approach you, even though they speak to you, remain quiet and unmoving until they pass.'

"So it happened. The man, with his family and belongings set out in the early morning. Suddenly they distinguished the outlines of soldiers rapidly approaching. They turned aside from the road and stood silent, tense.

"The soldiers hurriedly approached, and the poor man heard one of them shouting: 'Here they are, I see people here. Probably there is some nice booty for us there.'

"Another one laughingly answered him. "Friend, you probably slept poorly last night, since you cannot distinguish stones from humans. They are quite near us and you can see they are stones!"

"The first one insisted, 'But I even see a horse!" The other one laughed.

"On such a stony horse you will not ride far. Could you imagine that a horse, aware of all our horses, you remain immovable?"

"The soldiers all laughed heartily, and deriding the mistake of the first one, passed quite close to the unmoving group. Then they disappeared into the mist. Thus, even in the most difficult situation the man was saved. For he had been useful to Shambhala just once.

"Shambhala knows all. But the secrets of Shambhala are well guarded."

"Lama, how are the secrets of Shambhala guarded? It is said that many co-workers of Shambhala, many messengers, are speeding through the world. How can they preserve the secrets entrusted to them?"

"The great keepers of mysteries are watching closely all those to whom they have entrusted their work and given high missions. If an unexpected evil confronts them, they are helped immediately. And the entrusted treasure shall be guarded. About forty years ago, a great secret was entrusted to a man living in the Great Mongolian Gobi. He was told that he could use this secret for a special purpose, but that when he felt his departure from the world approaching, he should find someone worthy to whom to entrust his treasure. Many years passed. Finally this man became ill, and during his illness, an evil force approached him and he became unconscious. In such a state, he could not, of course, find anyone worthy to whom to entrust his secret. But the Great Keepers are ever vigilant and alert. One of them from the high Ashram hurriedly started through the Gobi, remaining more than sixty hours in the saddle without rest. He reached the sick man in time to revive him, though only for a short time; it permitted him to find someone to whom he might transmit the message."

"Lama, in Tourfan and in Turkestan they showed us caves with long, unexplored passages. Can one reach the Ashrams of Shambhala through these routes? They told us that on some occasions, strangers came out of these caves and went to the cities. They wished to pay for things with strange, ancient coins which are now no longer used."

"Verily, verily, the people of Shambhala at times emerge into the world. They meet the earthly co-workers of Shambhala. For the sake of humanity, they send out precious gifts, remarkable relics. I can tell you many stories of how wonderful gifts were received through space. Even Rig-den-jyepo Himself appears at times in human body. Suddenly He shows Himself in holy places, in monasteries, and at a predestined time, pronounces his prophecies.

"By night or early morning before sunrise, the Ruler arrives in the Temple. He enters. All the lamps at once kindle themselves. Some recognize the Great Stranger. In deep reverence, the lamas gather. They listen with the greatest attention to the prophecies of the future.

"A great epoch approaches. The Ruler is ready to fight. Many things are being manifested. The cosmic fire is again approaching the earth. The stars are manifesting the new era. But many cataclysms will occur before the new era of prosperity. Again, humanity will be tested to see if the spirit has progressed sufficiently. The subterranean fire now seeks to find contact with the fiery element of the Akasha; if all good forces do not combine their power, the greatest cataclysms are inevitable. It is related how the blessed Rigden-jyepo manifests Himself, to give command to his messengers; how on the black rock, on the way to Ladak, the mighty ruler appears. And from all directions, the messenger-riders approach in deep reverence to listen; and in full speed they rush to fulfill what is ordained by the great wisdom."

"Lama, how does it happen that Shambhala on earth is still undiscovered by travelers? On maps you may see so many routes of expeditions. It appears that all heights are already marked and all valleys and rivers explored."

"Verily, there is much gold in the earth, and many diamonds and rubies in the mountains, and everyone is so eager to possess them! And so many people try to find them! But as yet, these people have not found all things—so, let a man try to reach Shambhala without a call! You have heard about the poisonous streams which encircle the uplands. Perhaps you have even seen people dying from these gases when they come near them. Perhaps you have seen how animals and people begin to tremble when they approach certain localities. Many people try to reach Shambhala uncalled. Some of them have disappeared forever. Only a few of them reach the holy place, and only if their karma is ready."

"Lama, you speak of a holy place on earth: Is there rich vegetation there? The mountains seem barren and the devastating frosts unusually severe."

"In the midst of high mountains there are unsuspected enclosed valleys. Many hot springs nourish the rich vegetation. Many rare plants and medicinal herbs are able to flourish on this unusual volcanic soil. Perhaps you have noticed hot geysers on the uplands. Perhaps you have heard that only two days away from Nagchu where there is not a tree or plant to be seen, there is one valley with trees and grass and warm water. But who may know the labyrinths of these mountains? Upon stony surfaces it is impossible to distinguish human traces. One cannot understand the thoughts of people—and he who can, is silent! Perhaps you have met numerous travelers during your wanderings—strangers, simply attired, walking silently through the desert, in heat or cold, towards their unknown goals. Do not believe, because the garment is simple, that the stranger is insignificant! If his eyes are half closed, do not presume that his glance is not keen. It is impossible to discern from which direction power approaches. In vain are all warnings, in vain are all prophecies; but only by the one path of Shambhala can you attain achievement— by addressing yourself directly to the Blessed Rigden-jyepo you can succeed."

"Lama, you said that the enemies of Shambhala would perish. How will they perish?"

"Verily they perish in due time. They are destroyed by their own nefarious ambitions. Rigden-jyepo is merciful. But the sinners are their own assailants. Who can say when the merited wage is given? Who can discern when help is truly needed? And what shall be the nature of that help? Many upheavals are necessary and they have their purposes."

"How are sinners annihilated? One lama painter had the exalted gift of painting the sacred images with incomparable beauty. Superbly he painted the images of Rigden-jyepo and the Blessed Buddha and Dukkar, the All-seeing. But another painter became jealous and in his wrath determined to harm the righteous one. And when he started to slander the lama painter, his house caught fire from an unknown cause. All his possessions were destroyed and the hands of the slanderer were seriously burned, so that he was unable to work for a long time.

"Another villain threatened to destroy all the labors of an honest man. And he himself was drowned shortly after while crossing the Tsampo. Another man, who performed many a beautiful deed for charity, was attacked by some-one who sought to destroy all the possessions which had been dedicated to the cause of humankind. But again, the powerful ray of Rigden-jyepo reached the assailant and in a day his wealth was swept away and he became a beggar.

Perhaps you may see him even now, begging at the Lhasa bazaar."

"In every city you may hear how those unworthy creatures that turned their venom against worthy ones were punished. Only by the path of Shambhala may you walk safely. Each diversion from this road of glory will embroil you in the greatest dangers. Everything on earth may be explored and measured. But neither faith nor blind worship does the Blessed One ordain, but the knowledge of experience."

SHAMBHALE LAM

(White Waters)

"I CAN tell how, from distant Altai, many Old Believers went to seek the so-called 'Belovodiye' (White Waters) and never returned. I have heard the names of the mountains, rivers and lakes which lie on the way to the holy places. They are secret; some of the names are corrupted, but you discern the fundamental truth.

"I can tell you how a worthy student of this exalted teaching set out to reach Shambhala before the time ordained for him. He was a pure and sincere spirit, but his karma had not been exhausted and his earthly task was still undone. It was premature for him, and one of the great Masters met him on horseback in the mountains and personally spoke to this aspiring traveler. Mercifully and compassionately he sent him back to complete his unfinished labors. I can tell you of Ashrams beyond Shigatse. I can tell you how the Brothers of Shambhala appeared in various cities and how they prevented the greatest human calamities, once humanity worthily understood them.... Lama have you met Azaras and Kuthumpas?"

"If you are familiar with so many incidents, you must be successful in your work. To know so much of Shambhala is in itself a stream of purification. Many of our people during their lives have encountered the Azaras and Kuthumpas and the snow people who serve them. Only recently have the Azaras ceased to be seen in cities. They are all gathered in the mountains. Very tall, with long hair and beards, they appear outwardly like Hindus. Once, walking along the Brahmaputra I saw an Azara. I strove to reach him, but he swiftly turned beyond the rocks and disappeared. Yet, I found no cave or fissure there—all I saw was a small Stupa. Probably he did not wish to be disturbed.

"The Kuthumpas are no longer to be seen now. Previously they appeared quite openly in the Tsang district and at Manasarowar, when the pilgrims went to holy Kailas. Even the snow people are rarely seen now. The ordinary person, in his ignorance, mistakes them for apparitions. There are profound reasons why, just now, the Great Ones do not appear so openly. My old teacher told me much of the wisdom of the Azaras. We know several places where these Great Ones dwelt, but for the moment, these places are deserted. Some great reason, great mystery!"

"Lama, is it then true that the Ashrams have been moved from the vicinity of Shigatse?"

"This mystery must not be uttered. I already said that the Azaras may no longer be found in Tsang."

"Lama, why do you priests claim that Shambhala is far beyond the ocean, when the Shambhala of earth is close? Csoma de Koros even mentions, with justification, the place—the wondrous mountain-valley, where the initiation of Buddha was held."

"I have heard that Csoma de Koros reaped misfortune in his life. And Grünwedel, whom you mentioned, became insane, because they touched the great name of Shambhala out of curiosity, without realizing its stupendous significance. It is dangerous to toy with fire—yet fire can be of the greatest use to humanity. You have probably heard how certain travelers attempted to penetrate into the forbidden territory and how these guides refused to follow them. They said, 'Better kill us'. Even these simple folk understood that such exalted matters may be touched only with utmost reverence.

"Do not outrage the laws! Await in ardent labor until the messenger of Shambhala shall come to you, amid constant achievement. Await until the Mighty-voiced shall utter 'Kalagiya.' Then you may safely proceed to discuss this superb matter. Vain curiosity must be transformed into sincere learning, into application to the high principles of everyday life."

"Lama, you are a wanderer. Where shall I find you once again?"

"I beg you, do not ask my name. Moreover, should you meet me in some city, or in any other inhabited place, do not recognize me. I shall approach you."

"And if I should approach you, would you merely depart or would you in some way hypnotize me?"

"Do not force me to utilize these natural forces. Among certain Red Sects, it is permitted to apply certain powers. But we may only utilize them in exceptional cases. We must not break the laws of nature. The essential teaching of our Blessed One bids us to be cautious in revealing our inner possibilities."

"Lama, tell me further if you have personally seen the Rigden-jyepo."

"No, I have not seen the Ruler in flesh. But I have heard His Voice. And during the winter, while the frost lay over the mountains, a rose—a flower from the far-off valley—was His gift to me. You ask me so much that I see you are grounded in many matters. What would you do, should I begin to examine you?"

"Lama, I should be silent."

The Lama smiled. "So you do know much. Perhaps you even know how to use the forces of nature, and how in the West during the last few years many signs were witnessed—especially during the war, which you, or one of you started."

"Lama, certainly such unprecedented slaughter of human beings must have precipitated an unprecedented flow of reincarnations. So many people died before the predestined hour and through such occurrences, so much was distorted and thrown into upheaval."

"Probably you did not know the prophecies by which these calamities were foretold long ago. If you had known, you would never have begun this horrible holocaust.

"If you know of Shambhala, if you know how to utilize

your latent natural forces, you must also know of Naming the Heavenly Letters. And you will know how to accept the prophecies of the future."

"Lama, we have heard that all the journeys of the Tashi Lama and the Dalai Lama were foretold in the prophecies, long before they occurred."

"I repeat that in the private apartments of the Tashi Lama, all the events of his future travels were painted at his order. Often unknown strangers report these prophecies, and you can see and hear evident signs of approaching events.

"You know that near the entrance of the great temple of Gessar Khan there are two horses—a white and a red one. And when Gessar Khan is approaching, these horses neigh. Have you heard that recently the great sign occurred and many people heard the neighing of the sacred horses?"

"Lama, you mentioned the third great name of Asia...."

"Mystery, mystery, you must not speak too much. Some time we shall speak to one very learned Geshe of Moruling. This monastery was founded by our Dalai Lama the Great, and the sound of the Great Name is part of the name of the monastery. It is said that before leaving Lhasa forever, the Great Dalai Lama had a mysterious communion in this monastery. Verily, from this monastery, several Lamas disappeared for great new tasks.

"There you could find something familiar to yourself."

"Lama, can you tell me something of the three greatest monasteries near Lhasa—Sera, Ganden and Depung?"

The Lama smiled. "Oh, they are great official monasteries. At Sera, among the three thousand Lamas, you can find many real fighters. Many Lamas of foreign countries such as Mongolia are in Ganden. There is the chair of our Great Teacher, Tsong-Kha-pa. No one can touch this great seat without trembling. Depung also has some learned Lamas."

"Lama, are there some hidden passages under the Potala? And is there a subterranean lake under the chief temple?"

The Lama smiled again. "You know so many things that it seems to me you have been in Lhasa. I do not know when you were there. It makes little difference if you were there now or in other garments. But if you have seen this subterranean lake, you must have been either a very great Lama, or a servant bearing a torch. But as a servant you could not know many of the things which you have told me." Probably you know also that in many places of Lhasa there are hot springs and in some houses, people use this water for their household.

"Lama, I have heard how some animals—deer and squirrels and jackals—approach the meditating Lamas in the caves of the Himalayan forests; the apes and monkeys sometimes bring them food."

"On my part, I shall ask you, what is impossible? But one thing is evident—that a deer would not approach a human being in a city because only rarely do you find well-intentioned people in these crowded places. Humanity does not know the significance and the definite effect of auras; they do not realize that not only human beings, but even inanimate objects have their significant and effectual auras."

"Lama, we know about it and we have even begun to photograph auras. And as for inanimate objects, Lama, we know something about the Chair of the Master, and how this Chair must not be touched by anyone. In this way, the presence of the Great Ones is always near."

"If you know the value of such a venerated armchair, then you know the meaning of Guruship. Guruship is the highest position we can attain in our earthly garb. We are guarded by Guruship and we ascend to perfection in our esteem to the Guru. He who knows the essential meaning of the Guru will not speak against relics. In the West, you also have portraits of dear ones and you have great esteem for symbols and the objects used by your forefathers and great leaders. So do not take it as idolatry, but only as a deep veneration and remembrance of the work performed by a Great one. And it is not only this external veneration, if you know something of psychical emanation from objects, then you also know about natural magic. What do you think of the magic scepter which indicates the subterranean riches of earth?"

"Lama, we know many stories everywhere about the strange power of this moving stick, through which many mines, springs and wells are located."

"And what do you think is at work in these experiments, the stick or the man?"

"Lama, I think that the stick is a dead thing, whereas man is full of vibration and magnetic power. So, the stick is only as a pen in the hand."

"Yes, everything is concentrated in the person. Only know how to use it, and how not to misuse it. Do you in the West know something about the Great Stone in which magic powers are concentrated? And do you know from which planet came this stone? And who possessed this treasure?"

"Lama, about the Great Stone we have as many legends as you have images of Chintamani. From the old Druidic times, many nations remember these legends of truth about the natural energies concealed in this strange visitor to our planet. Very often in such fallen stones are hidden diamonds; but these are nothing in comparison with other previously unknown metals and energies which are found every day in these stones and in the numerous currents and rays.

"Lapis Exilis, thus is named the Stone which is mentioned by the old Meistersingers. One sees that the West and East are working together on many principles. We do not need to go to the deserts to hear of the Stone. In our cities, in our scientific laboratories, we have other legends and proofs. Would anyone have thought that the fairy tales regarding the flying man would ever be fulfilled? Yet now, each day's mail, each day's visitor, may come by flying."

"Certainly the Blessed One said long ago that steel

birds would fly in mid-air. But at the same time, without having to lift such heavy masses we are able to soar in our subtle bodies. You Westerners always dream of ascending Mount Everest in heavy boots; but we reach the same heights and far higher summits without trouble. It is necessary only to think, to study, to remember and to know how to grasp consciously all one's experiences in the finer bodies. Everything has been indicated in the Kalachakra, but only a few have grasped it. You in the West with your limited apparati can hear sounds at long distances. You can catch even the cosmic sounds. But long ago, Milarepa, without any apparati, could hear all the supreme voices."

"Lama, is it true that Milarepa in his young days was not a man of spirit? Somewhere we have read that he even killed the entire family of his uncle. How, then, can such a man become a spiritually developed being after such excesses of wrath and even murder?"

"You are right. In his youth, Milarepa not only killed this family but probably committed many other heinous crimes. But the ways of the spirit are inexplicable. From one of your missionaries, we have heard of your Saint named Francis. Yet in his youth he also committed many offenses, and his life was not so pure. Then how could he in one lifetime attain such perfection as to make him esteemed in the West as one of the most exalted of saints? We have learned many tales from your missionaries who visited Lhasa in former centuries, and some of your books are in our libraries. It is said that books of your gospel may be found sealed in some of our Stupas. Perhaps we know better than yourselves how to venerate foreign religions."

"Lama, it is so difficult for us Westerners to venerate your religion, because so many things are confused, so many things are corrupted. For instance, how could a stranger, on seeing two monasteries completely alike in exterior, understand that in one Buddhism is preached, while the other is the bitterest enemy of Buddhism? Even if one enters these monasteries, one sees almost the same images superficially. Thus, for a stranger to distinguish whether or not a Swastika is turned in an inverse direction is as difficult as to understand why the same iconography can act for and against Buddha. It is difficult for an outsider to understand why people who are completely illiterate and given to drink are called by the same title of lama as yourself, who knows many things and is so deeply cultured."

"You are right. Many Lamas wear the lamaistic garment, but their inner life is far worse than that of a layman. Often among many thousands of Lamas, you can find only a few isolated individuals with whom you can converse about exalted matters and expect a worthy response. But is it not thus in your own religion?

"We have seen many missionaries—they may speak of the One Christ, yet they attack one another. Each one calls his teaching superior. It is my belief that Issa gave one teaching—then how can this great Symbol have divisions which declare themselves hostile to the others? Do not think that we are so ignorant. We have heard that rites celebrated by one sect of Christian priests are not recognized by other Christian priests. Therefore, you must have many opposing Christs.

"In our deserts, many Christian crosses have been found. Once I asked a Christian missionary if these crosses were authentic, and he told me they were spurious crosses; that during all ages, false Christianity had penetrated Asia, and that we should not regard these crosses as exalted symbols. Then tell me, how shall we distinguish the authentic cross from the false ones? We also have a cross in the Great Sign of Ak-Dorje. But with us, this is the great sign of life, of the fiery element—the eternal sign. Against this sign, none would speak."

"Lama, we know that only through the knowledge of spirit can we perceive what is authentic."

"Again, you show your knowledge of great things. Again you speak as though from our mighty Kalachakra. But how shall we develop our great understanding? Verily, we are wise in spirit; we know everything -- but how shall we evoke this knowledge from the depths of our consciousness and transmit it to our minds? How shall one recognize the needed frontiers between the ascetic and the mundane life? How shall we know for how long we may be hermits and how long we must work among men? How shall we know what knowledge can be revealed without harm, and what—perhaps the most exalted—may be divulged but to a few? This is the knowledge of Kalachakra."

"Lama, the great Kalachakra is practically unknown, because its teaching is confused with the low Tantric teaching. Just as you have real Buddhists and their opposites, Bon-Po, so you have the lowest Tantra, sorcery or necromancy. And did not the Blessed One denounce sorcery? Tell me frankly whether a lama should be a sorcerer?"

"You are right, not only sorcery but an undue display of supernatural forces was forbidden by our great Teachers. But if one's spirit is so advanced that he can perform many things and utilize any of his energies in a natural way and for the purpose of the Common Good, then this is no longer sorcery but a great achievement, a great labor for humanity.

"By our symbols, by our images and thankas, you may see how the great Teachers functioned; among the many great Teachers you see only few in complete meditation. Usually they are performing an active part of the great labor. Either they teach the people or they tame the dark forces and elements; they do not fear to confront the most powerful forces and to ally themselves with them when it is for the common well-being. Sometimes you can see the Teachers in actual conflict, dispersing the evil of spirit. Earthly war is not sanctioned by us, but Buddhists throughout all history have been attacked; they have never been the aggressors. We have heard that during your recent Great War, the Christian priests on either side claimed that Issa and God were with them. If God is One, we must understand by this that He was in conflict with Himself. How can you explain a contradiction which was so inexplicable to all Buddhists?"

"Lama, the war is over. The most disastrous of mistakes may happen, but now all nations are thinking of how to abolish not only the idea by the actual material and implements of war."

"And do you think that all guns and warships should be abolished? Let them rather be transformed into implements of peace and of a loftier teaching. I would like to see the great warships become traveling schools of higher learning. Is that possible? During my journey in China I saw so many guns and warships that I thought, if only these ghastly creations might be symbols of lofty teaching rather than symbols of murder, what a tremendous flow of cosmic energy the world would see!"

"Lama, the serpent stings, yet he is considered the symbol of wisdom."

"Probably you have heard the old parable of how the snake was cautioned not to bite, but only to hiss. Each one must be powerful—but which protection do you regard as the most powerful?"

"Lama, certainly it is the protection afforded by the power of the spirit, because only in spirit are we fortified mentally and physically. A person, spiritually concentrated, is as strong as a dozen of the brawniest athletes. The one who knows how to use his mental powers is stronger than the mob."

"Ah, now we once again approach our great Kalachakra. Who can exist without food? Who can exist without food? Who can exist without sleep? Who is immune to heat and cold? Who can heal wounds? Verily, only the one who studies the Kalachakra.

"The great Azaras who know the Teachings of India know the origin of Kalachakra. They know vast things which, when they will be revealed to help humanity, will completely regenerate life! Many of the Teachings of Kalachakra are unknowingly used both in East and West; even in such unconscious utilization, much that is wonderful results. Therefore imagine how incomparably great would be the possibilities manifested by conscious achievement, and how wisely the great eternal energy could be used—this fine, imponderable matter which is scattered everywhere and which is available for our use at any moment. This Teaching of Kalachakra, this utilization of the primary energy has been called the Teaching of Fire. The Hindu people know the great Agni—ancient teaching though it be, it shall be the new teaching for the New Era. We must think of the future; and in the Teaching of Kalachakra we know there lies all the material which may be applied for the greatest use. Now there are so many teachers—so different and so hostile to each other. And yet so many of them speak of the one thing that is expressed in the Kalachakra. One of your priests once asked me, 'Are not the Kabbalah and Shambhala parts of the one teaching?' He asked, 'Is not the great Moses an initiate of the same teaching and a follower of its very laws?' We may assert one thing only. Each teaching of truth, each teaching of the high principles of life, issues from the one source. Many ancient Buddhist Stupas have been converted into Linga Temples and many mosques bear the walls and foundations of ancient Buddhist viharas. But what harm is there if those buildings have been dedicated to the one lofty principle of life? Many Buddhist images upon the rocks find their origins in teachings which long antedated the Blessed One. Yet they also symbolize the same high Essence.

"What is revealed in the Kalachakras? Are there any forbiddances? No, the lofty teachings set forth only the constructive. So it is. The same high forces are proposed for humanity. And it is revealed most scientifically how the natural forces of the elements can be used by humanity. When you are told that the shortest way is through Shambhala, through Kalachakra, it means that achievement is not an unattainable ideal, but rather it is something which may be attained through sincere and industrious inspiration here, upon this very earth and in this very incarnation. This is the Teaching of Shambhala. Verily,

each one may attain it. Verily, each may hear the pronunciation of the word *Kalagiya!*

"But to attain this, a man must dedicate himself entirely to creative labor. Those who work with Shambhala,
the initiates and messengers of Shambhala, do not sit in
seclusion—they travel everywhere. Very often they perform
their works not for themselves, but for the great Shambhala; and they are without possessions. Everything is available to them, but they take nothing for themselves. Thus,
when you dedicate yourself to Shambhala, everything is
taken and everything is given to you. If you have regrets,
you yourself become the loser; if you give joyously, you
are enriched. Essentially the Teaching of Shambhala lies
in this—that we do not speak of something distant and
hidden. Therefore, if you know that everything may be
achieved here on earth, then everything must be rewarded
here on earth. You have heard that the reward of Shambhala is here and that it is manifold in its returns. This
is not because the teaching of Shambhala is unique from
others, but because it is vital; it is given for earthly incarnations and can be applied under all human conditions.
In what way can we learn to work? How to be ready for
all manner of attainments? How to be open and all accept-
ing? Only in the practical study of Shambhala. When you
read the many books about Shambhala, partially translated in other languages and partially veiled, do not be
confused about the great symbols. Even in the West, when
you speak of great discoveries you use technical language;
the layman does not understand it and takes the expressions literally, judging only on the surface. The same may
be said of the great scriptures and of scientific documents.
Some take the great Puranas in their literal aspect. What
conclusion may they draw? Only that which may be gathered from the surface of the language, from its philology,
but not from the significance of the signs which are used.
The harmony of exterior and interior can be attained only
through the study of the Kalachakra. You have probably

seen the signs of the Kalachakra carved in the rocks, in quite deserted places.

"Some unknown hand has set a design upon the stones or has chiseled the letter of the Kalachakra upon the rocks. Verily, verily, only through Shambhala, only through the teaching of Kalachakra can you attain the perfection of the shortest path.

"*Kalagiya, Kalagiya, Kalagiya!* Come to Shambhala!"

Then our conversation became still more beautiful and sacred. Into it entered that note which exalts all human strivings. We spoke of the mountain Kailas, of the hermits who even now live in the caves of this wondrous mountain, filling space with their evocative calls to righteousness.

And then we spoke of That Place which lies to the north of Kailas....

SACRED LAND

THE majestic grandeur of the Himalayas has furnished a mine of previous lore for all nations. Each country speaks of them in its own way, as the Sacred Land or the Abode of Wisdom. And India, which is the motherland of the Blessed One, knows that the ancient Rishis strengthened their spirit amid these marvelous regions.

There can be found their stronghold as well as the cave of Milarepa, and there, among the snow passes, stand the gigantic rock carvings of Maitreya. In the holy caves of Kailas is the Threshold of Miracle. The popular wisdom which attributes all knowledge and high achievement to the influence of the Himalayas has given these heights the most beautiful and poetic titles. There is the "Kanchendzo-na" (the Five Treasures of the Great Snow); the "Jomo-Kangkar" (the Snow White Queen, known as Everest); the "Jomolhari" (the Divine Summit of the Queen); the "Kang Rim-po-che" (The Precious Snow, known as Kailas); the "Nochin Kang Zang" (the Blessed Snow of Devas); the "Gon-po-ri" (the Summit of the Protector). It is the people—in their enthusiasm for all that is heroic and beautiful—that have given these majestic titles. The legends of the Himalayas are to be found from the Pamir to Lhasa, from the Kunlun to the Brahmaputra. To the north of the Rhotang Pass there is a region leading to Tibet and Central Asia known as the Plateau of the Dead. A footpath has recently been made, and near it, leading into the pass, is a flight of immense stone steps. Close by is Vyasa Kund where the Rishi Vyasa is said to have composed the *Mahabharata*. Some people affirm that this gigantic staircase was constructed by Gessar Khan, but others claim that it was built by Rigden-jyepo, the Ruler of Shambhala, when He defeated the enemies of the Sacred Land. To the south stand the ruins of the Palace of the Pandavas. To the west, remnants of a castle with a water tank carefully laid out can be seen on the mountain.

It is very strange, in the midst of the jungle, to come across a well-made tank or stone steps leading to where no one knows. According to ancient Chinese travelers there were, once upon a time, fourteen Buddhist monasteries in our Kullu Valley, not one of which has survived, and there are legends that Buddhist manuscripts have been buried near here which date from the time of Landharma. There are of course many legends.

Lamas often arrive here from Tashi Lumpo and since the flight of the Tashi Lama they have not returned to their native monastery. As the Tashi Lama himself reveres the legend of Shambhala, so do his followers praise this sacred conception. A lama once enquired of us: "Have you seen the thanka banner of the Ruler of Shambhala which depicts His fight against the powers of evil? When our Tashi Lama fled from Tibet, he took only a few banners with him, but among these were several which related to Shambhala. Many learned lamas fled from Tashi Lumpo, and a geshe, or learned painter, a gelong of Tashi Lumpo, recently arrived from Tibet. He knows how to paint the thanka of Shambhala. There are several renderings of this subject, but you should have the one with the battle in the foreground."

The lama then took up a position on a rug in the white gallery of our home and began to outline his complicated composition on specially prepared canvas

In the center appeared the Mighty Ruler of Shambhala amidst the glory of His majestic abode. Beneath Him waged a tremendous battle in which the enemies of the righteous Ruler were unmercifully destroyed. The banner was dedicated to "The illustrious Rigden King of Northern Shambhala."

It was quite touching to note with what respect and

veneration the lama set about his work, and every time he pronounced the name of the Ruler of Shambhala, he clasped his hands as if in prayer. In watching his work, I could not help noting how near it was to the Russian icon painters, both in technique and proceedings.

Not only from the Lamas do we hear of Shambhala, but it is also to be found mentioned in the Kalachakra of Atisha of the year 1027. Traces are likewise to be found at the Kumbum monastery, the home of Tzong-Khápa and in the Chinese monastery of Wu-tai-shan of which the head priest has written a remarkable book *The Red Path to Shambhala*, which has not yet been translated. In the Chumbi monastery there is an immense banner depicting the spiritual battle of Rigden-jyepo. Legions of faithful warriors from all parts of the world hasten to join in this great struggle for spiritual victory. Prjevalsky in his diaries hinted often at Shambhala, and similar allusions can be found in the writings of Csoma de Körös and Francke. Professor Grünwedel's translation of that ancient book *The Path to Shambhala* written by the Third Tashi Lama has aroused great interest in the West. Alexandra David Neel who has been to Tibet several times mentioned the myth of Gessar Khan whose legendary personality stands alongside that of Rigden-jyepo, with whom he is closely connected. In her article *The Coming Northern Hero*, Mme David-Neel says: "Gessar Khan is a hero whose next incarnation will take place in Northern Shambhala, where he will unite with his associates and leaders who followed him in his previous life. They will reincarnate in Shambhala, to which they will be attracted by the mysterious power of the Ruler or by those mysterious voices which are only heard by the initiate."

Gessar Khan, the Ruler, is coming with an invincible army to destroy evil and establish justice and prosperity in all lands. In Tibet, we were able to see how widespread such legends really are. We were told of the palace of Gessar Khan in Kham, where the swords of his army are collected for the crossbeams of his palace. The arrow is

the sign of Gessar Khan, and is said to be of lightning; the
tips which are sometimes found in the fields are said to be
crystallized thunderbolts. War is declared by the shooting
of an arrow, and we once saw a mobilization announced
by the dispatch of an arrow wrapped in red silk. In Leh
-- the capital of Ladak which is also the country of Gessar
Khan—there are many memories of him and of Shambhala, along with romantic songs and legends of the hero
and his wife Bruguma. High on the rocks you may notice
a white spot; you are told that this is a door leading to
the castle of Gessar Khan. On another rock we found the
image of a great lion also connected with the same hero.

Many ancient thanka paintings are dedicated to Shambhala. Before me, at the moment, are six paintings on this
subject. The most esoteric of these is a Mandala of Shambhala in which one can recognize certain allusions. At the
top is Yidam, a sign of elemental force, and an image of
the Tashi Lama, the author of The Path to Shambhala.
In the middle are snow white peaks arranged in a circle,
and one can distinguish three white borders. In the center
is a valley with many buildings and one can discern two
clefts which represent towers. On the tower is He Himself
whose light will shine at the predestined hour. Below one
can see Rigden-jyepo as the Commander of an immense
army engaged in a victorious battle. This is a new version
of the subject by the Geshe of Tashi Lumpo. On the lower
part of another painting we also see the image of a victorious struggle. In the midst, Rigden-jyepo Himself appears
giving His Commands. In front of the Ruler appear all
the lucky signs and treasures which are predestined to
mankind. Behind the Ruler is a palace and on either side
are His father and mother. Above is an image of the Buddha. This is a new version of the subject from Sikkim.
The third painting does not depict a battle but is triumphant with its golden decoration. In the center a large figure of Rigden-jyepo giving His blessing is shown. Before
him, the Ak-Dorje, or symbol of Lightning glows in gold.
Among the treasures below one can distinguish the triune

sign. At the top is the Lord Buddha and on the right and left, the third and last Tashi Lama. This picture is from Ghum. Another painting from Nagchu shows many warriors on horseback or on foot, commanders and councilors gathered around Rigden-jyepo. The fifth painting, which is from Tashi Lumpo, shows Rigden-jyepo giving the commandment of wisdom to several gurus. This thanka belongs to a series of ancient banner paintings, The Incarnation of the Tashi Lama. The sixth painting which was brought from Tashi Lumpo by a lama refugee shows an image of Rigden-jyepo Himself in the center. The back of the Ruler's throne has the aspect of blue wings surrounded by flowers. In His left hand He holds the Wheel of the Law and His right hand calls on the earth as a witness. Below one can distinguish all the nations of Asia according to their dress—Hindu, Chinese, Moslems, Ladakhis, Kalmucks, Mongols, Buryats and Tibetans. All of them bring treasures: one carries books, another arms, another flowers. In the midst the great Treasure can be seen. The battle is over and the nations have been called to peace and prosperity.

When one speaks of Tibetan art, people become skeptical and question whether there is really such a thing. Many imagine it to be a copy of Chinese art, but this is not altogether exact, and it would be better to define it as a fusion of Indian, Chinese and Iranian art together with other influences. It is exactly the blending of such influences that gives it a unique quality. On all this, Tibet has stamped the image of its wonderful mountain landscapes and its legendary lore, and the result is unlike any other art.

Tibetans have very vivid imaginations. One has only to observe their strongholds built high up like eagles' roosts to see their bold architectural genius.

Moreover, they possess a remarkable sense of color; wherever one observes a Tibetan sacred dance or procession, one is agreeably impressed by the gorgeous display of color.

Tibetan songs are also colorful and their gigantic trumpets have a victorious sound.

All these elements are reflected in Tibetan art, which possesses lofty qualities. And if it is a matter of influences, then the ancient Buddhist frescoes from the cave temples of Turkestan ought to be considered as imitative, although their original character makes them one of the greatest styles in art. In these frescoes, we can trace the great art of Ajanta, the art of the Iranian miniature, and the rare qualities of Chinese art—but fused in a marvelous manner and lifted to a great style by the genius of inspired artists and Buddhists. It is really very difficult to go into this question of origins, and one does not know at times what to think! Dr. George Roerich even found traces of the Greek myth of Polyphemus among the legends of Tibet.

Geographical and ethnographical peculiarities must of course be considered, and it is very important to distinguish where the seeds of Truth may be hidden. In Mongolia, China, among the Buryats, the Kalmucks and the Old Believers of Siberia one can discover traces of Shamanism and other religions. Everywhere one meets with veiled allusions to the legend of Shambhala. In the streets of Mongolian capital Ulan Bator, one can encounter detachments of the Mongolian cavalry singing a song of Shambhala with great emotion. They will tell you that Sukhi-Bator, the national hero of Mongolia and a leader in the recent movement for freedom, composed this song of Shambhala that was sung in all corners of Khalka.

It is a song that begins thus:

"Chang Shambalin Dayin,
    The war of Northern Shambhala!
        Let us die in this war
            To be reborn again
                As knights of the Ruler of Shambhala!"

Thus, even the latest movements in Mongolia are connected with Shambhala.

When I presented my painting of Rigden-jyepo, the Rule of Shambhala, to the Mongolian Government, it was accepted with great emotion; a member of the Government told me that they wished to build a memorial hall in which the painting would occupy the center.

One of the members of the Government said to me: "May I ask how you come to know of the vision which one of our venerable lamas had several months ago? The lama saw a great crowd composed of many nations all gazing toward the West. In the sky appeared a giant rider on a fiery steed surrounded by flames, bearing in his hand the banner of Shambhala. This was the Blessed Rigden-jyepo Himself and He bade the crowd to turn from the West towards the East. In the lama's description, the majestic rider looked exactly as he does in your painting."

Among the rocks near Mongolian monasteries you will often meet with the sign of the Three Treasures. Sometimes a steed will be seen bearing this sign, and the interpreters will whisper about the Kalachakra, about the great Treasure and about Shambhala. There are countless legends to be met with on this subject. In the desert, you may come across a lonely shepherd who is singing, but if you ask him to repeat the song, he will tell you that this song of Shambhala is only for the desert.

In Siberia, where there are Buddhist traditions of a northern type, you will find a peculiar interpretation of Shambhala; there, they will speak to you of Belovodiye—the Blessed Land. In the Altai mountains you may meet with a gray-bearded Old Believer; should he become friendly, he might tell you thus:

"From here you will proceed between the Irtysh and the Argun and after a hard journey, provided you do not lose your way, you will come to the salt lakes. This is a very dangerous road and many people have perished there. However, if you choose the right moment, you will be able to cross this dangerous region. Finally, you will reach the Bogogorshi mountains and from there come to the road to Kokushi, which is even more dangerous. After this, you must take the road over the Ergor itself and follow it until you reach the snowy land, and there, amidst the highest mountains is Belovodiye, the sacred valley. If despite all dangers your spirit is ready to reach this spot, the people of Belovodiye will greet you, and should they find that you are worthy, they may even permit you to remain with them. This rarely happens, however, and many people have tried to reach Belovodiye. Our grandfathers, Atamanov and Artomonov went there, and after disappearing for three years, managed to reach the sacred place. They were not allowed to stay there, however, and had to return. They told many wonderful things about this place and knew many more of which they were not allowed to speak."

In the salt lakes mentioned in this itinerary one recognizes the lakes of Tsaidam and their dangerous passes. Bogogorshi or Bogogoriye is the Burkhan Buddha mountain range and Kokushi refers to the Kokushili range. Ergor is the cold upland region of Changtang close to the Trans-Himalayas which lies in sight of the eternal snows. In 1926 we came across some people who had started out for Shambhala and had sent letters from that place.

Several Russian reviews have published articles on this subject in recent years.

The Journal of the Western Siberian Geographical Society in Omsk published an article in 1916 by Beloshinov—*To the History of Belovodiye*, and the Journal of the Russian Geographical Society in St. Petersburg published another article in 1903 by Korolenko entitled *The Journey of Ural Cossacks into the Belovodiye Kingdom.*

In these articles, we are told that the Old Believers' legend about Belovodiye, an earthly paradise where there are no persecutions, still exists. It is a mythical land lying somewhere in the East. Such legends arose toward the end of the 17th century, when persecutions of the Old Believers began in Moscovia. These Old Believers made great efforts to find this fairyland, and for some time, the Altai region came to be looked upon as Belovodiye, but gradually the legendary realm began to move in the direction of the Himalayas. The Old Believers also penetrated into India through Afghanistan.

Beloshinov's article recorded the story of such a journey told by an old man named Zyrianov who was still living in 1914, a story that had been sketched by the old man himself. In a newspaper of Perm in 1899, there was a story that somewhere in the East there exists a fairyland known as Belovodiye, to which an expedition of Cossack was dispatched in 1898. Then followed a detailed description of their hardships, but one thing particularly interested them—an image of Maitreya, the future Buddha, who held His fingers in the same posture as that in the images of the Old Believers.

I have before me at the moment an image of St. Josaphat (Bodhisattva) painted by the Tibetan lama Chompel. How many wonderful associations it evokes; how many set out on distant pilgrimages, once having heard of the glory of Buddhist strongholds! It was during the construction of the Buddhist temple in the Russian capital that I first heard of Shambhala. Being a member of the committee, I met with a very learned Buryat lama who was the first to pronounce the name Chang Shambhala.

It will be known someday why this name pronounced under such circumstances had a great significance. For the moment it will suffice to say that the name was pronounced in a circle of very learned people; since then, I have always paid special attention to it. I also remember our talks on this subject with our late friend Geshe Rimpoche of Chumbi. Not only did we meet him in Ghum and at our house in Darjeeling, but he also came to visit us here at Urusvati in the Kullu Valley. This venerable priest spoke much of Kalachakra and Shambhala, and also of the Venerable Devamitta Dhammapala. It was great pleasure for me to note with what esteem and friendliness the Tibetan spoke of the great Indian (Ceylonese) spiritual leader, and I recalled the legend of Atisha and Milarepa. "Verily", said our old friend, "only through the teaching of the Kalachakra and Shambhala can you attain the perfection of the shortest path." Then we spoke of the sacred mountain Kailas, of the hermits who lived in the caves there, filling space with their prayers for Good and Bliss.

Twilight fell and the room took on a fresh aspect. Above the head of Rimpoche hung of image of Chenrezi beautifully embroidered in fine silk, and it looked down at us meaningfully. Such images can no longer be found in Tibet. On either side was the image of Amitayus and the Lord Buddha, ever steadfast with the Dorje, the invincible sign of lightning, in His hand. From a shrine in the room, the White Tara Dolma smiled on us. A sense of fresh life emanated from a bunch of fuchsias and violet dahlias, and the image of the Invincible Rigden-jyepo reminded us of that mysterious place to the north of Kailas. In the corners of this banner were four significant images. Below was the successor of Rigden-jyepo with a Hindu Pandit, one of the first exponents of the Kalachakra. At the top were two images of the Tashi Lamas; on the left the Third Tashi Lama Panchen Palden Yeshe, who alluded to Shambhala, and on the right the last Tashi Lama, Panchen Cho-kyi nyi-ma ge-leg, namjyal pal-zang-po, who has issued several prayers to Shambhala. In the center of the banner was Rigden-jyepo Himself and from the foot of His throne radiated Ak-ojir, Ak-Dorje, the sign of Life.

Legions of people were gathered before the throne of Rigden. There was a Ladakhi with his black hat; Chinese in their round headgear tipped with red balls; a Hindu in white garments and a Moslem in a white turban. There were also Kirghiz, Buryats, Kalmucks and Mongols in their characteristic attire. Each of them brought the best gifts of his land. Not forced to do so, they came voluntarily from all parts of Asia to surround the great leader...not as conquered people. His hand pointed toward the earth with the majestic gesture of the great lion Sange, and upon the threshold of the earth, He gave His oath to build steadfastly. Blue clouds of incense rose toward the image, forming the characters of some mysterious language; but lest the great Truth be desecrated by the ignorant, the sign soon melted together and vanished into space.

An old man leads us to a stony hill and pointing at the stone circle of ancient tombs solemnly says:

"Here the Chud went under the earth. When the White Czar came to our Altai, and when the white birch wood began to bloom in our region, the Chud did not wish to remain under the White Czar. They went underground and closed the passage with mighty stones—there, can you see it? But the Chud did not go forever. When a new era will come, when the people from Belovodiye will return and give the people a new knowledge, then the Chud will return with their acquired treasures."

In Mongolia, we were not astonished to find many signs about Shambhala. In these countries the psychic powers are well developed.

When we approached Ulan Bator we had to stay one night at Iro. In the dark evening, we noticed fire on the other side of the river. We asked what it was, and received an unusual answer:

"There is a large monastery which is presently the cause of some widespread rumors throughout Mongolia. Last year near this monastery a wonderful child was born. When it was one year old, it gave an important prophecy about the future in plain Mongolian; afterwards it never spoke again, and was just an ordinary child."

Again a message about the future!

When we entered Ulan Bator, near a temple we saw an open place surrounded by a palisade, typical of Mongolian dwelling places.

"What is this?"

Again a surprising reply:

"This is a place for a temple of Shambhala; an unknown lama came and purchased this place for a future building."

In Mongolia there are not only many learned lamas who know about Shambhala, but even many laymen and members of the government can give the most striking answers to these questions.

When we spoke of the above-mentioned prophecies about Shambhala to a member of the Mongolian Government, he exclaimed with great surprise: "But this is the prophecy which was told by the boy on the Iro River! Verily, a Great Time is coming!"

And he told us how quite recently a young Mongolian lama in the region of Uliasutai had written a new book about Shambhala explaining the high meaning of Shambhala for the future, and speaking about the path to this wonderful place. Another highly intelligent Buryat, one of the Mongolian leaders, told us how a Buryat lama, after many difficulties, reached Shambhala and remained there a short time. About his unusual travels there were some striking details—it is told that when this lama and his guide reached the very frontier of the sacred valley, they saw a nearby caravan of yaks with salt. They were regular Tibetan merchants who unknowingly passed quite near the wonderful place. Even the air around it was so strongly charged that people cannot see what should not be seen.

Another detail was also striking. When this lama, on his way home from Shambhala, went through a very narrow subterranean passage, he met two men carrying , with great difficulty, a thoroughbred sheep that was needed for some scientific experiments to be conducted in the valley.

Many other wonderful things have been told by educated Buryats and Mongols. They speak about a mysterious light above Buddha, and of the miraculous stone, from a distant star, which has appeared in different places before great events. The Great Timur, it is said, temporarily possessed this stone. The stone is usually brought unexpectedly by unknown people. In the same way, it disappears, only to be manifested again after some time in another country. The main body of this stone lies in Shambhala, and a small piece of it is given out and wanders all over the earth, keeping its magnetic connection with the main stone.

Endless tales are told about this stone. It has been said that King Solomon and the Emperor Akbar also possessed

it. These stories remind us of the Lapis Exilis, sung by
the famous Meistersinger Wolfram von Eschenbach, who
closed his song with the line:

"Und dieser Stein ist Graal genannt!"
(And this stone is called the Grail!)

Also in Ulan Bator we heard from several sources about
the visit of the Great Mahatma Himself, the Blessed Rigden-jyepo, to two of the oldest Mongolian monasteries—
Erdeni-Dzo on the Orkhon River and Narabanchi.

We had already learned about the visit of the Mahatma
to Narabanchi from literature. But we were glad to see that
the same details were told by the lamas in remote Mongolia. It was told how once, about midnight, a group of
riders approached the gates of Narabanchi-Gampa. They
came from afar, their faces covered with fur. Their chief
entered the Gampa and all the lamps lit up at once. Then
he ordered that all gelongs and havarags should be called
together. He approached the chief place of Bogdogegen
and unveiled his face, and everybody present recognized
the Blessed One Himself. He told many prophecies about
the future, then they all mounted their horses and left as
quickly as they had come.

Another story about the arrival of the Mahatma of the
Himalayas to Mongolia was told to us by a member of the
Mongolian Scientific Committee. We recognized the story
told to us in India, which went as follows:

"As you know we have several lamas with great spiritual powers. Of course they do not live in cities or big monasteries; they usually live in remote khutons in mountain
retreats. About fifty or sixty years ago, one of these lamas
was entrusted with a mission which was to be carried out
by him alone; before his death, he was to entrust it to a
person of his choice. You know that the greatest missions
are given from Shambhala. But on earth they must be
carried out by human hands, under earthly conditions.
You must also know that these missions are carried out

despite great difficulties, which must be overcome by the strength of spiritual power and devotion. It happened that this lama partially completed his mission, but afterward became ill and lost consciousness; in this state he could not transfer the entrusted mission to a proper successor. The Great Mahatmas of the Himalayas knew of his difficulty. As the mission had to be carried out, one of the Mahatmas hurriedly undertook the long journey from the Tibetan uplands to the Mongolian plains. By riding for sixty hours straight, the Mahatma arrived in time. He cured the Lama temporarily, so that he was able to carry out his mission. You thus see how the Mahatmas are helping humanity, and what self-sacrifice and earthly challenges they take upon themselves to protect the Great Coming Cause."

In Mongolia, they named the Mahatmas "Great Keepers"; they did not know which of the Mahatmas had undertaken this journey, but in India they could not tell us with what purpose the journey had been undertaken.

Such are the ties of Asia. Who is bringing the news? What secret passages bring the unknown messengers? Facing the rather ordinary routine of everyday life, confronted with difficulties and rudeness and many unpleasant worries, in Asia you can never be sure that there is not someone knocking at your door with the most important news.

Two ways of life are evident in Asia, so don't be discouraged by the sights of everyday life. You can readily be rewarded with the Great Truth which will enwrap you forever....

Long journeys on camels.

In the air, the song of Shambhala is ringing again. In stony mountain passages and frozen uplands, you are never left without signs of Shambhala,

Our lamas bent over a stone slope. They collected on a nearby rock pieces of white quartz, and now they were carefully laying out something from these crystalline white stones.

What do these complicated designs mean? No, it is not a design—it is the monogram of Kalachakra. From now on, from far away, for all travelers, this white inscription will be visible—invoking the Great Teaching.

A day of Shambhala. A Festival. Many Mongolian guests. In front of the tent of Shambhala the lamas are praying for the Blessed Rigden-jyepo. A polished mirror is placed before a painted image of the Ruler. Water is poured onto the surface of the mirror from an ornamental vessel. The streams of water flow over the surface of the mirror and cover it with strange designs. The surface moves as if alive. This is a symbol of magic mirrors, where the future is revealed and where the runes of revelation are written.

A lama, a guide of the caravan, ties his mouth and nose with a scarf. Why? The day is not cold. He replies:

"Now some precautions are needed. We are approaching the forbidden lands of Shambhala. We will soon meet 'Sur'—the poisonous gas by which the frontier of Shambhala is guarded."

Our Tibetan, Konchok, comes riding up to us and says in a lowered voice:

"Not far from here, when the Dalai Lama went from Tibet to Mongolia, all people and all animals in the caravan began to tremble. The Dalai Lama explained that they should not be afraid; they had touched the forbidden zone of Shambhala whose vibrations were unknown to them."

From the Kumbum monastery a high lama came to visit us with his ornamented tent and colorful attendants. He gave us the sign of Shambhala. He told us that some Chinese recently asked the Tashi Lama to give them passports to Shambhala, which only he can do. And just now the Tashi Lama in China has published a new prayer, addressed to Shambhala. Now everything can be achieved only through Shambhala.

Again barren rocks, the desert.....

We are looking at one another in amazement. We all sensed a sudden strong perfume, as if from the finest incenses of India. From where does it come when we are surrounded by barren rocks? The lama whispers:

"Do you sense the fragrance of Shambhala?"

A suburgan of Shambhala is being built on the heights of Sharagol, near to Ulan Davan where the Mahatma rested on his way to Mongolia. All our lamas and we ourselves carry stones which we cover with clay and grass. The top of the suburgan is made of wood and covered with tin from gasoline cans; my paints are used for decorating. Lime is brought from the Humbolt mountains. The suburgan shines brightly in the purple of the desert. The Buryat lama paints many images and ornamentations in red, yellow and green. Local Mongols bring "Norbu-Rimpoche" their modest gifts: turquoise, corals and beads for inlaying into the suburgan. The high priest of Tsaidam himself comes to bless the consecration of the suburgan. The Mongols promise to guard this monument of Shambhala—if only the Chinese dungans or camels do not destroy it.

FRONTIERS OF SHAMBHALA

AGAINST the blue background of the desert hills, something white is shining. What can it be? Is it a huge tent? Is it snow? But there can be no snow at this time in the desert. And this white spot is too big for a tent. And why is it so sharply distinct from its surroundings? We approach. Coming nearer, it appears even larger than expected. It is a huge pyramid formed by the residue of a large geyser of glauber salt—a real fortune for a druggist. An icy cold salt spring flows from underneath this huge white mass. A lama whispers:

"This is the sign of the third frontier of Shambhala."

Coming nearer to the Brahmataputra you can still find more indications and legends about Shambhala. And a yet more tangible impression: In these regions, in the direction of Mount Everest, lived the seer—the hermit Milarepa.

Near Shigatse, on the picturesque banks of the Brahmaputra and nearer to the sacred lake Manasarovar, several ashrams existed quite recently. When you know this, when you know the facts that surround these wonderful places, you are enwrapped by a special feeling.

Traversing the Trans-Himalaya, you will discover not just one mountain range but a whole mountain country with a peculiarly complicated design of ranges, valleys and streams. At every step you will be convinced that the maps are only approximately correct. Because of their complexity, these regions will remain unexplored. The hermit hidden in a cave, the dwelling in a remote valley, can remain undisturbed.

Those who have personally wandered through these

labyrinths know that you come across the hidden, inaccessible places only by happy "chance."

Old volcanoes, geysers, hot springs and radioactivity present unexpected and pleasant discoveries. Often you can see a diversity of rich vegetation next to a glacier in a neighboring valley, apparently nourished by a hot spring. In the barren uplands of Dumbure we saw boiling springs and next to them magnificent vegetation. Strawberry, hyacinth and many other flowers were in bloom. There are several such valleys in the Trans-Himalaya.

While we camped in Nagchu, local people told us that there is a fertile valley bearing regular crops that can be found to the North of the Dangra-Yumzo lake, in the open stony upland some sixteen thousand feet high. Hot springs that supply a whole household may be found in some courtyards near Lhasa.

Having passed through such unusual uplands of Tibet with their peculiar magnetic currents and electric wonders, and having listened to witnesses and having ourselves witnessed them, we know about Shambhala.

When we followed the stream of the Brahmaputra, we remembered how a Tibetan representative in Ulan Bator advised us to visit an unusual hermit of great age; he lived in a mountain retreat, as he called it, several days west of Lhasa. The Tibetan insisted that the hermit was most extraordinary, for he was not a Tibetan according to what he knew, but a Westerner. Then we remembered how a respectable inhabitant of Sikkim told us of a strange hermit to the north of Kanchenjunga.

All eyes are attracted to the majestic white summits beyond the clouds, as if rising over an inferior world. From all lands, the highest hopes are directed to the Himalayas.

Kang-chen-zod-nga—Five Treasures of the Great Snow. And why is this gorgeous mountain so called? It is because it contains a store of the five most precious things in the world. What things?—gold, diamonds and rubies? By no means. The ancient East values other treasures. It is said that there will come a time when famine will overtake the whole world. At that time a Man will appear who will unlock the giant gate of these vast treasuries and will nourish all mankind. And it is of course understood that this Man will nourish humanity not with material food, but with spiritual food.

In ascending the Himalayas you are greeted by the name of Shambhala; in descending, the same great concept benefits you.

During our absence, our friend Rimpoche of Chumbi has built two more monasteries; everywhere the images of Maitreya and Shambhala are in a place of honor.

Our lama artist Lariva has painted a wall fresco—a Mandala of Shambhala in which, in a symbolically stylized way the secret valley is surrounded by snowy peaks and the Ruler, Rigden-jyepo is the central figure.

During these years, Geshe Rimpoche has begun to speak more openly of Shambhala. In symbolic form he tells of the power of the epoch of Shambhala.

Rimpoche presented a recently-published book dedicated to Shambhala to us. In this book, the prayers to Shambhala given out by the Panchen Rimpoche, the Tashi Lama, during his last travels, have been gathered. From this collection you can see that the Spiritual Ruler of Tibet made a special prayer to Shambhala wherever he stayed during his journey.

And then came the ring with the seal of Shambhala.

A revered gray Ghur from the Kullu Valley told us:

"In the Northern Land—in Utrakan—on the high uplands there live the great Gurus. Ordinary people cannot reach this land. The Gurus Themselves do not leave the heights at present—They do not like the Kali-Yuga. But in times of need They send Their pupils—chelas—to warn the Rulers of nations." Thus in the ancient sites of Kullu, the knowledge of the Mahatmas is crystallized.

Now let us summarize these scattered indications about Shambhala. The Teaching of Shambhala is a Teaching of Life. As in the Hindu Yogas, this Teaching shows how to use the finest energies that fill the macrocosm, energies which can be as mightily manifested in our microcosm.

Therefore are the Azaras and Kuthumpas related to Shambhala? Yes.

And the Great Mahatmas and Rishis? Yes.

And the Warriors of Rigden-jyepo? Of course.

And the whole cycle of Gessar Khan? In certain parts.

And Kalachakra? Yes.

And Aryavarsha, whence from where the Kalki Avatar is expected? Yes.

And the Ming-ste? And the Great Yarkhas? And the Great Holders of Mongolia? And the dwellers of Kalapa? And the Belovodiye of Altai? And Shabistan? And the valley of Lao-Tsin? And the Black Stone and the Grail—Lapis Exilis? And the Chud, the subterranean? And the White Island? And the underground passages of Turfan? And the hidden cities of Cherchen? And the submerged Kitesh? And the suburgan of Khotan? And the White Mountain? And the sacred valley of Buddha's Initiation? And Dedjung? And the book of Utaishan? And the Place of the "Three Secrets"? And the White Burkhan?

Yes! Yes! Yes! All these have assembled around the Great Name of Shambhala from many nations and many ages...these, as well as the whole mass of separate facts and indications, deeply felt inwardly, even if not completely expressed outwardly. Shambhala, or the White Island, is indicated to the West of Himavat. One notes the care and reverence with which the approximate locality of this remarkable sanctuary is given out.

Bhante-Ul and Dedjung are also synonyms for the White Island.

To the north of Kailas, towards Kuen-Lun and Cherchen, there was the so-called Aryavarsha from where the Kalki Avatar was expected.

"The Place of the Three Secrets", "The Valley of the Initiation of Buddha"—all these indications bring the consciousness of the people to the same direction, beyond the white ranges of the Himalayas.

Shambhala itself is the Holy Place where the earthly world links with the highest states of consciousness. In the East they know that two Shambhalas exist—an earthly and an invisible one. Many speculations have been made about the location of the earthly Shambhala. Certain indications put this place in the extreme north, explaining that the rays of the *aurora borealis* are the rays of the invisible Shambhala. This attribution to the north is easily understood— the ancient name of Shambhala is Chang-Shambhala, which means the Northern Shambhala, is explained as follows: the Teaching originally was manifested in India— where everything coming from beyond the Himalayas is called the North.

Several indications, couched in symbols, have put the position of Shambhala in the Pamir, in Turkestan or the Central Gobi. Wessel in *Jesuit Travelers in Central Asia* refers to the Jesuit Casella, who died in 1650 in Shigatse. Casella, who had unusually friendly relations with Tibetans, was invited by somebody to visit the land of Shambhala.

The many misconceptions about these geographical locations of Shambhala have quite natural reasons. In all books on Shambhala, in all oral legends, the location is described in the most symbolic language, almost undecipherable to the uninitiated.

For instance, take the translation by Professor Grünwedel of *The Path to Shambhala*, the famous book written by the Third Tashi Lama. You will be overwhelmed by the quantity of geographical indications, veiled and scrambled, so that only great knowledge of old Buddhist places and of local names can help you to somehow disentangle the complicated web.

SHAMBHALA—MONSALVAT

LAMA Champel tells us that in Kalimpong there is an ancient Tibetan book of the 18th century, in which the name of Prester John is mentioned, and in which it is said that Shambhala, at that time, was in Spain. The lama was astonished when George showed him the snapshots of designs of the Grail in caverns, which were recently discovered not far from Montserrat.

In 1933, an Austrian scientist stumbled upon the book of Parsifal Namak, probably of Manichean origin while studying ancient Persian manuscripts. The Templars knew these oral traditions from the Manicheans whom they met during the Crusades. The Albigensians were in touch with the same sources. Montserrat, Monsalvat, legendary until now, have become real by the recent investigations of a young Swiss scientist. The song of Wolfram van Eschenbach about the stone Grail becomes scientifically significant. Here are some more extracts from Mongolian oral traditions:

"When Hushi-Khan, the leader of all the Olets finished his fight with 'Nimava', he brought a magic black stone which was given to the Dalai Lama by the 'Lord of theWorld'. Hushi-Khan wanted to build the main city of the Yellow Teaching in West Mongolia. But the Olets, who at that time fought with the ruler of the Manchurs for the Chinese throne, were completely routed. The last Khan of the Olets, Amursana, fled to Russia, but shortly before that, he sent 'the black stone' to Ulan Bator.

When the stone arrived in Ulan Bator and the 'Living Buddha' blessed the people with it, the Mongols and their cattle were saved from illness and misfortune. But a hundred years ago, the stone was stolen. Buddhists searched for it all over the world, but in vain. From the moment of its loss, the Mongolian people began to die out."

It is remarkable how the most diverse people are interested in this legend. Although poor in its conception, "Shangri-La" was a successful film all over the world and was even translated into Chinese. Are there not more documents in the Vatican? The letters of Prester John were kept there. Are all of them published? It is instructive to watch the movement of the legends; lately the historical significance of legends and myths is being realized. Many valuable archaeological discoveries have been based on the study of legends. Where is the dividing line between the tale and the narration? Where is the dividing line between the dream state and the facts?

The true, unprejudiced science will examine and evaluate the truth.

TIBET

"THE grandeur of nature in Asia reveals itself in the endless forests and tundras of Siberia; in the waterless deserts of overwhelming grandeur; in a wide flat upland which forms the southern half of the central part of this continent." Thus does Prjevalsky speak of Tibet.

Everything that is said about Tibet is full of significance, whether it be by Plano Carpini, or Rubruquis, or Marco Polo, or Odoric of Friuli, or any of the many other travelers. They all saw some of the unusual in Tibet, and Tibet has remained as an unusual place.

It is said the Lhasa will now have a radio. Roads for automobiles are being mentioned, as well as airstrips. In other words, an interesting mystery is being approached from all sides. It is long since Waddell attempted to tell us about Tibet, but he did not say very much; Mme David-Neel said more, but primarily stressed the tantric side.

At present, many countries are divided as if into two distinct existences. One is mechanical, robot-like, technocratic—contained within the conventional bounds. Machines are climbing the mountains, and above the highest peaks hover airships; various apparati, more or less exact, calculate and measure; paper is substituted for precious metals. In other words, the old bazaar has become a modern bazaar with all its "improvements." And yet in all these newly technological countries, the old country also remains with its fundamental treasures, achievements and strivings intact.

In our day, the world's demarcation lines are very unclear. There was a day when one could speak of regressors and innovators; there was a time when the Stone Age was clearly followed by the Bronze Age. But now every-thing has become much more complicated. The Stone Age has contacted the Iron Age; regressors have absorbed the mechanical conventionality, while innovators have loving-ly contacted the ancient wisdom. For this reason, in tech-nological countries, it is only with difficulty that one can draw the lines of demarcation.

In Tibet, the radio will make its voice heard and the mountain air in many places will be polluted by the facto-ries. And yet Tibet—The Unusual—will remain.

We have just spoken of hidden things; there may be many types of things hidden. We have met visitors from remarkable places who have never noticed anything.

There once existed a game in which the players unex-pectedly asked each other: "What do you see?" And the unprepared answers were at times very strange. People usually noticed what seemed to be insignificant nonsense, and the simple game sometimes became an interesting psychological exercise.

If people would notice everything significant, no doubt a great many more treasures would have been studied on earth. And yet it is only now that the Roman Forum is being studied; only now Egypt, Palestine, Greece and Iran open up their treasures. And what shall we say of other, less frequented places: Even the kremlins are as yet unex-plored. Known frescoes have not as yet been studied in detail. And how much has been passed by unrecognized, as yet unnoticed!

Technocracy is especially strong at present. It has cal-culated everything on paper; but as soon as it contacts actual life. Its most exact formulas are drowned in the midst of non-applicability. In everyday life the telephone rings unbearably; the howling of jazz music drills the brain; the noise of the prizefight resounds. And yet, all this commonplace triviality does not affect that Unusual, that extraordinary, to which the human heart is striving.

We have seen people who were deeply disappointed not

only by Tibet but also by India, Egypt and the entire East. Just as unlucky travelers cannot see the radiance of the mountain peaks on misty days, so also were these travelers not fortunate enough to contact the places and circumstances of importance. One can see the beautiful historical Paris, but one can also see it in its repelling modern aspect. You many see one New York, or you may see its most unattractive quarters.

These two aspects—often mutually exclusive—are everywhere. Thus, there is nothing to fear that the Tibetan uplands—unusual as they are—will become vulgar. Even now, in some Tibetan bazaars there is nothing extraordinary except colorful folk products. How can one penetrate beyond these appearances? Of course, the language is needed; but the mere physical language is not in itself sufficient. One must possess an inner language; if it is found, much will be revealed, but if it is not found, then no concordance will result.

It is said that especially in the Orient this language of the heart is required... but, no doubt it is necessary everywhere. No matter with what technology people may cover themselves, they will always converge and separate along other paths... paths which—through the Tibetan uplands, through the highest mountains—will always remain unusual.

The statements of wise travelers over many centuries must certainly have a foundation. These self-sacrificing searches were real experiences. Many of their statements remain fully convincing. The diaries of these travelers are even now read with great attention, so accurately did they record that which they saw and experienced.

Franke reported that beyond a certain place in the Himalayas the guides refused to go, stating that beyond those mountains there was something unusual; this serious scientist recorded this statement in full earnestness. And we find similar statements by that remarkable man of the past—Prjevalsky.

The new Dalai Lama has still not been found—it has been an unusually long period. One remembers the great fifth Dalai Lama. No one knows of the last years of his life, when and whither he went. How unusually secret was his departure! This too lends to the mystery of Tibet.

LIGHT IN THE DESERT

S OUNDS in the great desert.
    The conch shell resounds. Do you hear it?
The long, lingering wistful call vibrates, quivers, melts into the chasms.

Is there perhaps a monastery or a hermit?

Here we have reached the most deserted spot. There is not one dwelling within six days from here. How can there be even one lama in these desolate mountains to sound his call?

But it is not a lama. We are in the mountains of Dunbure, and from times beyond memory this signified: "The Call of the Conch Shell."

Far off, the mountain call fades away. Is it reechoing among the rocks? Is it the call of the Memnon of Asia? Is it the wind whistling through the crevices? Or is a mountain stream somewhere gurgling? Somewhere this enticing, lingering call was born; and he who named these mountains "The Call of the Conch Shell" heard the summons of the sacred desert.

"White Chorten" is the name of our campsite. Two mighty masses form great gates. Is this not one of the boundaries? White signs.... white pillars of the dripping geysers...white stones. These boundaries are known. Around us, from out of the death mounds of avalanches emerge rocky crags. It is evening.

Above us lies another mountain pass. We must examine this site. It is from here we heard the conch shell. A short ascent; between two natural turrets, like cones, is an opening; and beyond is a small circular plain, protected like a fortress on all sides by sharp rocks. There is abundant grass upon this square, and under the rocks gleams the silent ribbon of a rivulet. Here is the very place for a camp...one can hide long and securely within this natural castle.

"Look.... something moves there...people!" whispers our fellow-traveler as his eyes peer through the evening mist.

Through a curtain of fog it seems as if a spectacle of phantoms is passing. Or was it a sound that intrigued our imagination? Were these perhaps swift antelope noiselessly leaping by? Gazelle and antelope are almost unnoticeable against the rocks. Perhaps someone, preceding us, coveted this unapproachable site. But all is serene. In the dusk the grass seems not to rustle. The sounds and whispers slumber for the night. The fires flare up in the camp. For whom shall they serve as a guiding star?

Again fires. The shadows dance. The tents merge into darkness. People seem to have multiplied. The men and camels seem numberless. Heads of camels and horses appear. The heat is immense; it is time to rest. The arms are laid aside and one forgets that this is the very site of the looting of caravans. Only one month ago, a caravan bound for China was destroyed in this place.

It is long since our men have seen trees. It is long since they felt the caress of tall grass. Let the fires of peace glow.

A rifle shot sharply pieces the silence! Our rest is broken. "Put out the fires!" Guards—form a file! Watch the tents. Two men with rifles, to the horses!" Konchok will reconnoiter. If there is peace, he will sing the song of Shambhala; if there is danger, a shot!

Once again a quiver passes through the camp and all becomes still. The row of riflemen take their places in the tall grass. Between the trunks of Karagach, the tents disappear as though submerged. A whisper—"Perhaps it is the men of Ja-lama, his bands are still active. His head, impaled on a spear, was taken through all the bazaars but his centurions wander the length of the Gobi. You—in the rear—listen! Is that the grass rustling?"

Suddenly out of the darkness comes the song of Shambhala. Konchok is singing. Somewhere, far off, the voice is heard. It means there is no danger. But the guards still remain at their posts and the fires are not lit. The song comes nearer. Out of the rustling grass the dim figure of Konchok appears, and he laughs:

"Stupid Chinese. He was alarmed at out bonfires, and he fired a shot in order to frighten us. He thought we were robbers. And he himself is riding a white horse!'

A Chinese caravan was going from Kara-Khoto to Hami, with a hundred camels and but one rifle. The Chinese guard mistook our fires for the bonfires of Ja-lama and wished to frighten us. He himself was completely terrified. He repeatedly asked if we were peaceful people and pleaded that we stay away from his caravan at night. Then this caravan became noisy and merry little fires started to twinkle, fire being the sign of confidence. Nevertheless, the watch increased and a password was given: "Shambhala", and the countersign: "Ruler, Rigden."

"Arragan", cries out lama Sange, as he reins in his horse. Between two hills in the morning mist appears the outlines of galloping horsemen with a spear and long rifles.

Now they are surely here! There are the same fifty horsemen of whom we were warned by the unknown well-wisher who came galloping to us from the mountains. Our road is intercepted; the attack will begin from the hill. Our forces are divided. The Torguts—our best shots—are far behind. Konchok and Tsering are with the camels. There are also Tashi and the other Konchok from Kokonur. But behind us is a hill, a high one. If we succeed in reaching it, we can gain a commanding position over the entire site, and there we can gather our forces. The enemy approaches the next hill in groups, but we waste no time; we reach the hill and are prepared. Osher and Dorje ride out to meet the enemy and wave a hatik. Osher calls out and his Mongolian address is heard far around. He calls:

"Beware of touching great people! If someone dares, he will feel the power of mighty arms which can demolish an entire city in ten minutes." The Panagis huddle together in a group; they listen to Osher and count our arms. Even our lama, Malanoff, has put a spade into his gun case and threatens them. The counting of arms is in our favor. The Panagis do not dare an open battle. They lower their rifles; only one long spear, as before, remains aloft.

"Can you sell this spear? I wish to buy it." Our enemy smiles. "No this spear is our friend. We cannot part with it." Afterwards I heard that this spear was a sign of war and that riders leave their yurtas only in case of hostile intentions. Our enemy, finally deciding to abandon hostilities, begins to relate a long story about a lost white horse for which they are searching. This story is a familiar one, for in other parts of Asia suspicious strangers would also begin a story about a lost horse, thus hiding their original intentions.

When we spread our tents, we saw how the herds were being driven home from the mountains to the far off yurtas. This was also a characteristic sign that a battle had been decided upon.

Strange riders went to the mountains, in different directions. Did they ride to retrieve their hidden possessions, or to summon new allies?

One must be ready for unexpected events and one's arms must always be at hand.

Toward evening when the bonfires of peace were already lit, some of our "enemies" came to the camp with a special interest in our firearms. With astonishment we learned that this wild tribe knows such words as Mauser, Browning, Nogan, and were discussion in depth the quality of our rifles.

Again, they went back and nobody knew their final decision. But they asked us, under various pretexts, to stay there one more day. Who knows; perhaps this was in expectation of some help on their side.

In spite of the peaceful fires of the camp, we took measures against a night attack. Dugouts were made on two points in the soft sandy ground to defend the camp from two sides. The watch was increased and a post was assigned to every person, to be occupied in case of alarm.

Before dawn, we discovered the loss of a few camels. After a long search they were found in a very strange place between the rocks. Perhaps it was hoped that we would depart, disappointed at being unable to find our animals.

The sun was already setting when we moved toward the pass, with guards flanking both sides of our caravan.

Again, strange armed riders rode past us. They dismounted from their horses and stood with their long rifles. Some of our men also dismounted and paraded before them with their rifles ready.

Passing a stony way we came to this pass, and suddenly we heard two rifle shots in the far distance. Later, on the edge of the mountains, we saw our vanguard with his rifle over his head. This was a sign of warning. We again took position and two of our men with field glasses approached the danger zone. After several minutes, we saw a signal— "no danger."

When we came near, our vanguards were still looking through the field glasses. One of them insisted that something had happened; probably one of our Torguts and a horse were shot. But the other noticed that our mule detachment was proceeding without any obstacles and behind it was a black mass containing several figures below the pass. This must be free of danger.

Descending the pass, we saw in the distance huge herds of wild yaks—several hundred heads—so typical of the mountains of Marco Polo. By now, it was apparent to us that the black mass was a huge yak, which had been shot and was being skinned by our Torguts.

But the danger of an attack had not completely vanished. Our Mongols insisted that the Panagis would not attack us near their yurtas, fearing that in case of defeat their yurtas would be set on fire. But beyond the pass, in a far more isolated spot, there would be greater possibility of an attack. The Mongolian lama Sange was so frightened by these suggestions that he approached us with a white hatik in his hand and begged our leave that all Mongols depart and return at once to their homes. But we did not accept the hatik and this unpleasant discussion remained unresolved.

Coincidentally, assistance was on its way to us. Out of season for September, it had been thundering for some time in the mountains; our Mongols whispered that the powerful god, Lo, was very angry at the Panagis for their evil motives. After the thunder and lightning, heavy snow began to fall, which was most unusual for that time of year. The courage returned to our Mongols and they shouted: "You see the wrath of the gods! They are helping us! The Panagis never attack in snow, because we could retaliate by following their tracks!"

Nevertheless, our camp was a gloomy one. Through the blizzards the fires burned but dimly and the voices of the sentinels sounded faintly.

I recall another stop, also around bonfires, but other fires were seen in the distance. These are the camps of the Golloks. The entire night they shout: "Ki-ki-no!" and our horpas answer: "hoho hey!" By these distance calls the camps announce to each other that they are vigilant and ready to fight. It means nothing that at sunset the men were still visiting each other, for with the departure of the sun and with the moon in sway, the mind may also change. And suddenly the fires of peace are extinguished.

Again a snowfall. Huge sharp rocks surround the camp, casting gigantic shadows. Around the fire sit some huddled figures. Even at a distance you see one of them lifting up his arms, and against the red streams of fire you see his ten fingers. He is ardently recounting something. He counts the innumerable army of Shambhala. He speaks about the unconquerable weapons of these legions -- about how the great conqueror, the Ruler of Shambhala Himself, leads them. How no one knows whence they come, but they destroy all that is unjust. And behind them follow the happiness and prosperity of the countries. Messengers of the Ruler of Shambhala appear everywhere. As if in response to this tale, a gigantic shadow appears on the opposite rock! And some person, all golden in the rays of the fire, descends from the mountain. Everybody is ready for exalted news. But he who comes is a yak driver. Nevertheless he brings good news: the yaks for Sanju Pass are ready. Good news! But the charm of the fairytale is gone. With disappointment they throw new tar roots into the fire.

And the fire hisses and sinks again. On a gilded yellow stone, surrounded by the violet mountains with snowy white peaks, under the dome of a blue sky, they sit closely. On the long stone something shiny, brightly colored, is stretched out. In a yellow high hat, a Lama is relating a story to an attentive listener, while with a stick he points to something which is illustrating his story. The brightly colored picture is an image of Chang Shambhala. In the middle there is the Ruler, the Blessed Rigden-jyepo, and above him Buddha. Many magnificent offerings and treasures are displayed before the Ruler, but His hands do not touch them and His eyes do not seek them. On the palm of His hand, stretched out in blessing, you can see the sign of high distinction. He is blessing the humanity of the future. He is on His watchtower helping the good and destroying the sinners. His thought is an eternal, victorious battle. He is the light destroying the darkness. The lower part of the picture shows the great battle under the guidance of the Ruler Himself. Hard is the fate of the enemies of Shambhala. A just wrath colors the purple blue clouds. The warriors of Rigden-jyepo, in splendid armor with swords and spears, are pursuing their terrified enemies. Many of them have already fallen and the firearms, big hats and possessions are scattered upon the battlefield. Some of them are dying, destroyed by the just hand. Their leader is already smitten, and lies spread under the steed of the great warrior, the Blessed Rigden. Behind the Ruler, on chariots, follow fearful cannons which no walls can withstand. Some of the enemy, kneeling, beg for mercy, or attempt to escape their fate on the backs of elephants. But the sword of justice overtakes defamers. Darkness must be annihilated. The point of the lama's stick follows the course of the battle.

In the silence of the desert evening, seated around a bonfire the sacred history of the Victory of the Light is related. Ten fingers are not sufficient to indicate the number of the legions of Shambhala. No hyperbole is adequate to describe the might of the Lord of the World.

Amidst the all-conquering frost, the bonfires seem meager and without warmth. The short period from eleven to one o'clock seems somewhat warmer, but after one o'clock, the frost is augmented by a sharp wind and the heaviest fur coat feels no warmer than light silk. For the doctor there is a wonderful possibility to observe the extraordinary conditions of altitude. Mme Roerich's pulse reaches 145, or as the doctor says, becomes as that of a bird. Instead of 64, which is my normal pulse, I have a pulse of 130. One's ears ring, as if all the cicadas of India were gathered together. We are attacked by snow blindness. This is followed by an extraordinary sensation: the eye sees everything double and both images are equally strong. Two caravans, two flocks of ravens, a double silhouette of the mountains.

Our doctor prophesies that with such frosts, the heart, already exhausted by the altitude will begin to get weaker, and during the coldest nights, a man may fall asleep forever.

The doctor writes another medical opinion: "Further detainment of the expedition will be considered an organized attempt on the lives of its members."

Early one morning, when the sun had just touched the highest summits, the doctor came in quite excited, but satisfied, exclaiming: "There you have the results of our situation! Even brandy is frozen! And so, all that lives may become frozen and quiet forever." He was told: "Certainly, if we desire to freeze, we shall be frozen. But there is a remarkable thing, like psychic energy, which is warmer than fire and more nourishing than bread. The chief thing in cases like this is to preserve our calm, because irritation deprives us of our best psychic weapon."

Naturally, I do not blame the doctor for his pessimism; the usual medicines do not have good results in such unusual conditions. Moreover, the chief medicine of his supplies, strophantus, has run out. And he could produce only an empty bottle of adonis vernalis, the other needed medicine,.

Fuel is almost impossible to obtain. For a bag of argal the inhabitants of the black tents demand large sums of money. And each one prefers some special coins. One requires old imperial Chinese taels; another insists on coins with a figure—a dollar from Sinkiang; the third wants money with the head of Hun-Chang and seven letters; and still another desires this same coin with six letters. One person will sell only for silver Indian rupees. But nobody accepts American or Mexican dollars, nor the Tibetan cooper sho, despite its imposing inscription: "The government Victorious in all directions."

But what gives warmth to the modest bonfires? In spite of an indescribable cold, ten fingers are again uplifted. First they are lifted to count the frozen caravans, and then to enumerate the numberless armies of sacred warriors which shall descend from the Holy Mountain to erase all criminal elements. And during these stories of fiery battles, of the victory of righteousness over the dark forces, the bonfires begin to glow and the ten uplifted fingers apparently cease to feel the cold. Bonfires of the cold.

A black mass moves quickly up a very steep rock. Wild yak herds of at least three hundred heads flee from the caravan. Our Mongolian shooters, preparing their rifles, try to slow up and remain behind the caravan; but we know their tricks. Although they are Buddhists, and around their necks and even on their backs they have incense bags and small caskets containing sacred images, above all they are shooters, hunters—and great is their desire to send a sharp shot into the black mass of fleeing yaks. The hunters stop.

"Osher, Dorje, Manji, listen, you must not shoot! You have food in abundance!"

But does a hunter shoot for food? Far away on the flint stone plains a black mass can be seen again. It is even larger and more dense. There is something awe-inspiring in such a large herd of wild yaks. This time, the Mongols themselves advise us to take a side path and go around the herd, which they estimate at a thousand yaks. And there may be very old and fierce ones among them.

But as regards to hunting kyangs, the Mongols are unrestrainable. Fines were levied in camp for every unnecessary shot, and also for willful absence from camp. But what can one do when a hunter, despite this, disappears behind a neighboring hill and returns some two hours later with a bloody skin of a kyang thrown over the rump of a horse and with pieces of meat, hastily cut from the carcass, hung all around the saddle? They are just like the Hunn horsemen carrying their meat under their saddles. All smeared with blood, the hunter smiles. Whether or not you punish him, his passion is satisfied. And the other Buddhists also disapprove of your prohibition of killing animals. They all simply delight at the thought of having fresh meat of yaks or kyangs roasting over their evening fires.

An antelope pursued by a wolf runs right into the caravan. The riflers, under restraint, watch covetously. But if people can be restrained, you cannot restrain the dogs, and the poor antelope soon finds itself between two fires. However, the wolf is also frightened of the caravan and turning aside, takes off, jumping instead of leaping. But the antelope will escape the dogs. Even the mountain hen and small wild goats make fools of the Mongolian dogs, and lead them far away from their young ones.

And here are the bears! Dark brown with wide white collars. At night they come quite close to the camp, and if it were not for the dogs, they would satisfy their curiosity calmly, without any thought of escape, even by day.

Now we move along the riverbed of the clear Burengol. Under the hooves of the horses, blue copper oxide shines like the best of turquoise. Above us is a steep rock and at the very edge of it is a huge bear that keeps pace with our caravan, watching us curiously. Who will touch him, and for what?

But certain animal species have become real enemies of the caravan. Those are the marmots, the tabagans and the shrew-mice. The whole district is undermined by their innumerable burrows. Despite the greatest care, the horses often slip, and at once they are up to their knees in these underground cities. Not a day passes without a horse slipping into the treacherous excavations of these burrowers.

At the evening, the Tibetan Konchok brings two mountain pheasants to the bonfires. How he caught them barehanded remains a riddle. One need hardly guess who it is that wants to kill and eat them, but there are also voices for their release. We again turn to the Buddhist covenants and after some bargaining, we exchange the birds for a Chinese tael. And a minute later, the free prisoners gaily flit away towards the mountains.

The fox hunts mountain partridge: a kite watches a hare; the dogs zealously chase marmots. The animal kingdom lives its own law. A recent episode regarding the animal kingdom concerned three hens. From Suchow, we had taken with us a cock and two hens, and the latter dutifully presented us with eggs every day, notwithstanding the turmoil of their daily voyage. However, when there was nothing left with which to feed the fowl, we presented them to a Tibetan officer. Someone's observant eye noticed the absence of the hens and he immediately reported it to the governor. A very lengthy correspondence was started regarding whether we had eaten the three fowl. In fact, there were letters to Lhasa about it!

Once again, by the light of the night bonfires, our shaggy Tibetans assembled and blinking to each other, told the latest gossip from the neighboring dzong, and as usual, derided their governor. And the same warming fire, which just before had been the scene of inspired narratives about Shambhala, now illuminated the faces condemning the officials of Lhasa.

The lamas consecrate a suburgan in the name of Shambhala. In front of the image of Rigden-jyepo they pour water on a magic mirror; the water runs over the surface of the mirror, the figures become blurred as in the ancient stories about magic mirrors. A procession walks around the suburgan with burning incense and the head lama holds a thread connected with the top of the suburgan, wherein various objects of special significance have been placed. There is an image of Buddha, there is a silver ring with a most significant inscription, there are prophecies for the future and there are the precious objects: 'Norbu-rimpoche'. An old lama came from the neighboring yurtas and brought a small quantity of 'treasures'—a piece of mountain crystal, a small turquoise stone, two or three small beads and a shiny piece of mica. The old lama had taken part in building the suburgan and he brought these treasures with the insistent request to place them in the opened shrine. After a long service, the white thread that connected the head lama and the suburgan was cut, and in the desert the suburgan remained, protected only by invisible powers. Many dangers threaten these shrines. When caravans stop for a rest, the camels spoil the edges of the base; curious sheep jump on the cornices and try the strength of the picturesque images and ornaments with their horns. But the greatest danger comes from the Dungan Moslems.

The Mongols have a saying: "If a suburgan can resist the Dungans, then it is safe for the ages." Around the bonfire, stories are told of the destruction of Buddhist sanctuaries by Dungans. It is said that the Dungans light fires in old Buddhist caves which are decorated with ancient murals, in order to burn and destroy these frescoes with smoke. The people, with terror in their eyes, tell how in the Labran Province Dungans demolished the statue of Maitreya himself. Not only did they persecute the Buddhists, but also the Chinese followers of Confucius. The Mongols say that although it is difficult with the Chinese, the Dungans are worse still—they are absolutely impossible. They are regarded as inhuman, cruel and bloodthirsty. One remembers all manner of atrocities that took place during the Dungan uprising. One sees ruins on every hill and everywhere there are stones in formless heaps. In the minds of the people almost all these remnants are somehow associated with the Dungans. Here was a fort built by the Dungans; here was a village burnt by the Dungans; and that gold mine died after the Dungans passed through it; there was a well which the Dungans filled with sand in order to deprive the place of water.

A whole evening was devoted to these horrible stories. And around the bonfire one could see again the ten raised fingers, this time recounting the cruelty of the Dungans.

The bells on the camels of the caravan are of different sizes, and they sound like symphony. This is an essential melody of the desert; during the day, the heat kills everything. Everything becomes still, dead. Every creature creeps into the coolness of the shadow. The sun is the conqueror and is alone on the immense battlefield. Nothing can withstand it. Even the great river, even Tarim himself, stops flowing. The burning stones are as claws of agony until the conqueror disappears behind the horizon, seeking new victories. Darkness does not care to reappear. Only a bluish mist covers the expanse, without beginning and without end. To this bluish symphony, what type of melody might be fittingly added?

The chiming of bells is soft as old brass and rhythmic as the movement of ships in the desert. This alone can complete the symphony of the desert; and as a counterpoint, you have a mysterious song accompanied on the zither by the untiring hands of the baksha—the traveling singer. He is singing about Sabistan, about fairies which come from the highest planes down to the earth to inspire the giants and heroes and the beautiful sons of kings.

He sings about Blessed Issa, the Prophet, who walked through these lands and about how he resurrected the giant who became the benevolent king of this country. He sings about the holy people behind this very mountain and about how a holy man could hear their sacred chants, even though they were six months distant from him. In the stillness of the desert, this baksha joins the bells of our caravan. A holiday is being held in the next village, and he is going there to present his sacred art and to relate many stories about any number of wonderful things that are not a fairy tale, but the real life of Asia.

The first camel of the caravan is adorned with colorful carpets and ribbons, and a flag is placed high above his load. He is an esteemed camel; he is the first. He takes the responsibility of filling the desert with his ringing, and he steps forward proudly. His black eyes seem to know many legends.

But instead of a baksha with holy songs, a rider overtakes us. And high penetrating notes pierce the space. This is a heroic Chinese song.

I doubt whether you can ever hear these heroic and sometimes Confucian chants in the European quarters if the harbor cities of China. But in the desert the feeling of ancient China, of the Chinese conquerors of immense spaces, penetrates the heart of even the contemporary amban (governor). The rhythm of the camel bells is broken. The hooves of the horse of the amban are thundering. And the large red tassel is waving on the neck of a big Karashar horse, gray with stripes like a zebra. Another tassel is hung on the breastplate of the horse. Under the saddle there is a large Chinese sword. The points of the rider's black velvet boots are curled upward. The stirrups have gilded lions, and the adornment of the saddle is complex. Several rugs soften the long ride. From Yarkend to Tun-huang it is a two-month journey to follow the ancient Chinese road where jade and silk and silver and gold were transported by the same riders, with the same bell, swords and songs. Noisily, the amban with his retinue joins us. The camels are behind and the horses are inspired by hordes of the grandsons of Ghengis Khan.

A small city. Another amban comes out of his yamen, surrounded by a fenced wall, to greet our Chinese traveling companion. Both potentates greet each other with great ceremony. It is like something out of an old Chinese painting. They are so glad to see each other as they hold each other's hands and enter the large red gates. Two black silhouettes in the sandy-pearl mist, guarded by two armed warriors, are painted on both sides of the clay wall.

* * *

"Allah! Allah! Allah!" shout the Moslems, preparing for Ramadan when they fast during the day and can eat only after nightfall. And to avoid falling asleep, they fill the air around town with their shouts and songs.

But quite another shout is to be heard from the vicinity of a great tree. Two Ladakhis of our caravan are singing prayers dedicated to Maitreya. So the songs of all religions are gathered around one bonfire.

* * *

On old stones throughout the whole of Asia are to be found peculiar crosses and names, written in Uighur, Chinese, Mongolian and other tongues. What a wonder! On a Mongolian coin is the same sign! In the same way have Nestorians crossed the desert.

Moving sands. Like miserly guardians they defend the treasures which sometimes appear on the surface. Nobody dares to take them because they are guarded by unseen forces and can be given out only at a predestined time. Poisonous essences are spreading from the earth. Do not lean over the ground, do not try to take from the ground what does not belong to you. Otherwise you will fall dead, as falls the robber.

An experienced rider sends a dog before him, because the dog will first feel the influences of these earthly essences. Even an animal will not dare to enter the forbidden zone. No bonfires will attract you in these hidden places. Only vultures will fly high over the mysterious land. Are they also not guardians? And to whom belong the bones which glimmer so whitely on the sands? Who was this intruder who dishonored the predestined dates?

Again, around the bonfire ten fingers are raised and a story, convincing in its simplicity and reality, uplifts the human heart. Now the story is about the famous black stone. In beautiful descriptive symbols, the old traveler will tell the awed audience how, from time immemorial, from some other world, a miraculous stone fell down—the Chintamani of the Hindus and Norbu-rinpoche of the Tibetans and Mongols. Since those times, a part of the stone has been traveling on earth, signaling the new era and great world events. They tell how some ruler possessed this stone and how the forces of darkness tried to steal it.

Your friend, listening to this legend, will whisper to you: "The stone is black, 'vile' and 'fetid' and it is called the origin of the world. And it springs up like a germinating thing—so dreamt Paracelsus." And another of your companions smiles: "Lapis Exilis, the Wandering Stone of the Meistersinger."

But the narrator of the fire continues his tale about the miraculous powers of the stone and how, by all sorts of manifestations, the stone is indicating events and the very nature of existence.

"When the stone is hot; when the stone quivers; when the stone cracks; when the stone changes its weight and color—by these changes the stone predicts to its possessor the future and gives him the ability to know his enemies and dangers, as well as happy events."

One of the listeners asks: "Is not this stone on the tower of Rigden-jyepo, whose rays penetrate all oceans and mountains for the benefit of humanity?"

And the narrator continues: "The black stone is wandering on the earth. We know that a Chinese emperor and Tamerlane possessed this stone. And authoritative people say that the great Suleiman and Akbar had it in their possession and through the stone, their might was augmented. This stone is called "Treasure of the World."

The bonfires are burning like old fires of sacrifice. You enter your tent. All is calm; in the usual surroundings it is difficult to imagine something unreal, even unrepeatable. It is dark in the tent, then suddenly out of your fingers a flame leaps and rushes through all objects touched by you, not harming them. Again you have come in contact with some inexplicable combination of currents. This occurs only on the heights.

The bonfires were not yet fully lit when a shot resounds in the twilight. Who is shooting? Tashi has killed a snake. What a strange snake, with a sort of beard with black and gray markings!

Around the fire long stories are told about snakes. One Mongol tells:

"If somebody does not fear the snake, he should grab it by the tail and shake it hard. And the snake will become as stiff as a stick until you shake it again."

My companion was bending down to me:

"You remember the Biblical staff of Moses, how he manifested a miracle when the staff was transformed into a snake. Maybe he used a cataleptic snake and with a powerful gesture returned her to life."

Many Biblical signs are to be remembered in the desert. Look at these huge pillars of sand which suddenly appear and move for a long time as dense masses. This miraculous pillar, which moved before Moses, is so clearly envisioned by one who knows the desert wanderings—and again you remember the burning and unburnable bush of Moses. After seeing the unceasing flame in your tent, such a bush for you is no longer an impossible miracle, but a reality that lives only in the desert. When you hear how the great Mahatma traveled on horseback for the fulfillment of urgent high missions, you also do not wonder, because you know of the existence of the Mahatmas. You know their great wisdom. Many things which absolutely cannot find a place in the life of the West, are becoming simple here in the East.

There are still more Biblical echoes. On the very summit of a mountain several stones can be seen. Some ruins, probably.

"This is the former throne of Suleiman", explains the leader of the caravan to you.

"But how does it happen that throughout Asia thrones of Solomon are to be seen everywhere? We have seen them in Srinagar, near Kashgar; there are several in Persia."

But the caravaneer does not give up his idea. "Certainly there are many thrones of the great king Suleiman. He was wise and powerful. He had an apparatus to fly all over many lands. Stupid people think he used a flying carpet, but learned men know that the King possessed an apparatus. Though it could not fly very high, still it could move in the air."

So again, something of the way of the traveling is revealed, but the old flying carpet has been abandoned.

In the same way, the stories of the conquests of Alexander the Great are confused. On one side, the great conqueror is linked with Gessar Khan; in another version, he is the Emperor of India. But quite an elaborate myth is attributed to Gessar Khan which tells about the birthplace of the beloved hero. There are romantic descriptions of his wife Bruguma, his castle, and his conquests, which were always for the benefit of humanity. Quite simply, a horpa will tell you about a palace of Gessar Khan in the Kham Province, where the swords of his innumerable warriors were used in place of beams. Singing and dancing in honor of Gessar Khan, the horpa offers to procure one of these unconquered swords. Sand and stones abound, and yet the idea of unconquerability is alive.

In Europe, when you hear about a city of a robber-conqueror, you think perhaps of the old tales of Spain or Corsica. But here in the desert, when you hear that your

next stop will be before the walls of the city of the notori-
ous Ja-lama, the bandit of Central Gobi, you are not the
least bit astonished. You only look over your arms and
ask what kind of attire is most suitable for the encounter: European, Mongolian or Sartian. During the night
you hear dogs barking and your men say calmly: "These
are the dogs of the men of Ja-lama. Ja-lama himself has
already been killed by the Mongols, but his band has not
scattered as yet." During the night, in the red flames of
bonfires, you can again see the ten fingers. This time, the
stories are about the awe-inspiring Ja-lama and his cruel
companions. How he stopped large caravans, how he took
many people captive and how hundreds of these involun-
tary slaves worked on the construction of the walls and
towers of his city, which gave life to the solitude of the
Central Gobi. It is told in what battles Ja-lama was victorious, what supernatural powers he possessed, how he
could give the most terrorizing orders, and how they were
executed at once. How, following his orders, ears, noses
and hands of disobedient ones were cut off, and the living
witnesses of his terrible powers were set free.

In our caravan there are two who personally knew
Ja-lama. One is Tsaidamese, who was fortunate to escape
from captivity. The other is a Mongolian Lama, an experienced smuggler, who knows all the secret paths in the
desert—paths unknown to anyone else—along with hidden
streams and wells. Was he not at one time a co-worker of
Ja-lama? He smiles:

"Not always was Ja-lama a bad man. I have heard how
generous he could be. You only had to obey his great forces. He was a religious man. Yesterday you saw a large
white suburgan on a hill. His prisoners were ordered to
assemble these white stones together. And whoever was
protected by him could cross the desert in safety."

Yes, yes, this lama probably had something to do with
this late illustrious bandit. But why should a simple bandit build a whole city in the desert?

In the first rays of the sun we saw a tower and part of

a wall behind the next sandy hill. Our party, with carbines ready, went to explore the place because our caravaneers insisted that some of Ja-lama's men might be lurking behind the wall. We stayed and looked through our field glasses, but after an hour, George appeared on top of the tower, the sign that the citadel was empty. We sent to inspect this city and found that only the spirit of a great warrior could have outlined such a building plan. Around the citadel we saw many traces of yurts, because the name of Ja-lama attracted many Mongols who came to live under his protection. But later they scattered after having seen the gray head of the former leader on a spear in the Mongolian bazaars.

Ja-lama probably hoped to live long in this place, because the walls and towers were solid and his house was spacious and well-defended by a system of walls. In an open field of battle, the Mongols could not conquer him. But a Mongolian officer came to his place, apparently for peaceful negotiations. And the old vulture, who always penetrated all sorts of ruses, was this time blind. He accepted this mission and the bold Mongol arrived, carrying a white hatik in his hands; but behind the hatik was a Browning pistol ready to be used. Thus he approached the rule of the desert with an honorable offering, and shot him straight through the heart. Everything must have been dependent on the strong hypnotic power of Ja-lama, for strange to say, when the old leader fell dead, all his followers were gone at once in great commotion so that a small detachment of Mongols could occupy the citadel without a battle.

Behind the walls we could see two graves. Were they the graves of the victims of Ja-lama, or did one contain the decapitated body of the leader himself?

I remember how, in Ulan Bator, I was told a long story about the speculations which arose about the head of Ja-lama. It had been preserved in alcohol and so many wanted this peculiar relic that, after changing hands many times, it disappeared. Did it bring luck or sorrow to its possessor? Nobody knows the real psychology of Ja-lama who had a law degree from a Russian university and afterward visited Tibet, being for some time in personal favor of the Dalai-Lama. One thing is evident: his story will augment the legend of the Gobi and for many years it will be magnified and adorned with the flowers of Asian fantasy. For a long time to come, the ten fingers will be raised in front of glowing bonfires. The flames of the bonfires are glowing.

* * *

But there are moments when the bonfires of the desert are extinguished.

They are extinguished by water, whirlwind and fire.

Studying the uplands of Asia, one is astonished at the quantity of accumulated loess. The changes on its surface are most surprising. Often a relic of great antiquity is exposed; at the same time, an object of recent times is covered over with a heavy accumulation. In Asia, one must take this issue of surprises into account. Where are those gigantic streams which carried vast quantities of stone and sand, completely filling ravines and changing the profile of the entire district? Perhaps all these are only catastrophes of long ago.

The sky is covered with clouds. In the neighboring mountains at night, in the direction of Ulan-Davan, a strange dull noise constantly fills the space. And not once, or twice, but for three entire nights you awaken and hear this strange symphony of nature and do not even know if it is friendly or hostile. But in these vibrations there is something attractive, compelling you to listen attentively.

A gray day begins. Light rain. During the daily commotion you do not the mysterious tremor of the night. People are busy with customary conversations; their thoughts are concerned with the near future. They are preparing to sit at their usual dinner on the shore of a tiny stream, around which peaceful marmots live.

But another wonder of Asia is soon upon us. Through a broad chasm from the mountain tops a current rushes, overflowing the high banks of the stream, turning suddenly into a gigantic, storming river. It floods a large area. Yellow, foaming waves, full of sand catch some of the tents and whirl them away like wings of butterflies. From the depths of the waves, stones are leaping up at your very feet. It is time to think of saving yourself! Horses and camels, sensing danger, rush up the mountain. Cries are heard from the distant Mongolian yurts that stand in the valley as the current floods and demolishes the well-built yurts. What can withstand this power? The tents are destroyed, many things are carried away. The current rushes through transforming everything into a slimy swamp. Twilight brings a cool, unfriendly night followed by an equally cold morning.

The sun illuminates a new site. The stream has already settled into new banks. Before us there are lifeless, sloping hills, newly created by the power of the stream. In one night, our things have become deeply embedded in the new soil. Digging them up, one imagines the formation of the strata of Asia. What surprises they present to an investigator, who finds the prehistoric mixed with the contemporary! The fires, extinguished by the stream, slowly begin to burn the drying branches and roots anew. Not only water extinguishes the fires, but the great fire itself brings destruction to this peaceful area.

The steppe is burning. Local people hasten to depart. We too rush away from these dangerous parts. Horses feel the danger and tense their ears, harkening to a whirling, rumbling noise. A yellow wall, covered with black rings of smoke, is moving on. What an unexpected noise accompanies the leaping flames!

Looking at the wall you recall how Mongolian Khans and other conquerors of Asia used to set a fire to the steppe, deciding thus the destiny of battles. But of course the fiery element sometimes turned against the creators of the fire themselves. Your fellow traveler measures the distance to the flames with calm Mongolian eyes and talks quietly, as of the most usual thing:

"I think we will succeed in departing in time. We must reach that mountain," pointing to a far-off hill.

The next morning you observe the burned steppe from the mountain top. All is black, all has changed. And again, the layers of dust shall come and cover the black carpet. But you see smoke on the next mountain. What is it? A Mongol explains to you—there under the ground, coal has been burning for many months. Thus the Mongol calmly speaks of the destruction of his own treasures.

The whirlwind, too, extinguishes the bonfires. After midday, a gale begins. The Mongols cry out: "Let us stop, otherwise we will be carried away by the wind!" Sand and stones fly in the air. You try to hide behind the boxes of the caravan. In the morning it appears that you are standing on the very shore of a lake.

Various are the miracles of the desert.

And other fires, not bonfires, are glowing in the far distance. They are yellow and red. These mysterious sparks create complex structures. Look, there are cities of red sparks, some rising to create walls and palaces. Is that not a gigantic sacred bull glowing in the red-violet light? Are there not, in the far distance, several windows sparkling and inviting the traveler? From the near darkness, large black holes are emerging; ancient flat stones surround you as in an old cemetery. Under the hooves of horses, something strong and firm rings out like glass.

The Tsaidam guide says severely: "Walk, all of you, one after the other without turning from the path. Caution!" But he does not explain the reason for the caution and he does not want to go first. And the other Mongolian lama also does not wish to walk in front.

Some danger is lurking near. For one hundred and twenty miles we walk steadily without a halt. There is no water for the horses. In the early dawn we see that we are walking on a rather thin crust. In it, holes expose bottomless black salt water. These formations are not the slabs of a cemetery, but of salt. Maybe they will become tombstones for those who carelessly fall into the gaping black pit. What metamorphosis took place in these regions? The flaming castles disappeared with the coming of light. But when this peculiar seeming cemetery ended, we again saw around us yellow rosy sands.

Then came a story.

Once upon a time, a large city stood on this site. The inhabitants of this city were prosperous and lived at ease, surrounded by great wealth. But even silver gets dark when not used. So the accumulated treasures were not used properly, and the good principles of life were forgotten. But there is justice when the great patience is exhausted, and the unworthy are destroyed. The city was destroyed by fire, the air rent with cries and screams; this city suddenly plunged down and the sea filled the gigantic cavern. Much time has passed, and again the sea was covered with salt, but this site still remains uninhabited. All places where injustice has been manifested will remain uninhabited.

And the guide asks you with a mysterious look: "Perhaps during the night you saw some strange lines in the darkness?" One of our fellow travelers whispers: "Is this not a story of Atlantis? Is not Poseidon revealed in this legend?" But the guide continues: "Some of the people of this city, the best ones, were saved. An unknown shepherd came from the mountains and warned them of the coming disaster. And they went to the caves. If you wish, you may go to these caves. I will show you a stone door which is tightly closed. But we do not know how to unlock it."

"Do you also know where are the sacred frontiers which you never dare to cross?"

"Yes, only those who are called can enter those boundaries. There are some signs indicating these forbidden regions. But even without visible signs you can feel it because everyone who approaches will feel a tremor in his entire body. A hunter was sufficiently strong to cross this boundary. There he saw some miraculous, wonderful things, but when he tried to speak about the hidden matters, he lost his senses and became mute. With sacred matters we must be very careful. Everything revealed before the destined date involves a great calamity."

In the distance some shiny white peaks are emerging. There are the Himalayas! They seem not so high because we ourselves are on the heights. But how white they are! They are not mountains, but realms of snow. That is Everest, says the guide.

Nobody has as yet ascended this sacred treasury of shows. Several times 'pelings' have tried to conquer this mountain; some of them perished in the effort, and others had many hardships. This mountain is predestined for the Mother of the World. Its summits must be pure, unviolated and virgin. Only She, the Mighty, can be there, the Silence guarding the world.

The bonfires are glowing with the highest thoughts gathering around the flames. In the far desert, thousands of pigeons live among the sacred old tombs. Like holy messengers, they fly around and invite the travelers to the hospitable roof.

Around the bonfires, their white wings glimmer. The light in the desert.

Near the stream, over the precipice, the silhouette of a horse becomes faintly visible in the mist. And something seems to glitter strangely on the saddle. Perhaps this is a horse that has been lost from a caravan. Or perhaps this horse has thrown its rider while jumping over an abyss. Or perhaps this is a horse left behind because he was weak, and now looks for his master.

So speaks the mind, but the heart remembers other things. The heart remembers how from the great Shambhala, from the beautiful mountain heights at a destined hour, there will descend a lonely horse and on its saddle, instead of a rider, there will shine forth the jewel of the world: Norbu-rimpoche—Chintamani—the miraculous stone, preordained to save the world.

Has the time not come? Does the lonely horse not bring us the jewel of the world?

TRI-RATNA!

MAITREYA

"Peace to all Beings"

ON a piece of palm bark, with a sharp stylus, a friend-ly Bhikhu is writing in Singhalese. Is he berating anyone? Is he writing an appeal? No. With a smile he is sending a greeting to the far-off lands beyond the seas. A greeting to the good, benevolent people. And he does not expect a reply. It is simply a benevolent arrow sent into space.

In Kandy, in the ancient capital of Lanka-Ceylon, we are guided along the old traces of the past: The Temple of the Holy Tooth, the Temple of Para-Nirvana, wondrous treasury of sacred books in their hammered-silver bind-ing-boards. "And what is there in the small closed tem-ple?"

"That is the temple of Maitreya, the Lord of the Future."

"May one enter?"

The guide smiles and shakes his head benignly. "In this temple none may enter, save the chief priest."

Thus, the radiant future is not contaminated! We know it lives. We know its symbol is Maitreya, Metteya, Maitri—Love, Compassion. Upon this luminous sign of all-under-standing, all-inclusiveness, the great future is being built. It is pronounced with the most reverent solemnity. It must not be defiled or blasphemed by light-mindedness, curi-osity, levity and doubt. The *Vishnu Purana*, and all other *Puranas*—that is, all the ancient scriptures—speak in their highest expressions of the luminous future which human-ity serves, each individual in his own way.

Messiah, Maitreya, Muntazar—a glorious succession of names which, in diversity, has expressed this same sacred and heart-filled striving of humanity. With special exultation, the prophets speak of the future. Read all the passages of the Bible where the highest hopes of the people are expressed. Read the Teachings of Buddha about Maitreya. See how gloriously the Moslems speak of the Prophet of the Future.

How beautifully India speaks of the end of the Black Age of Kali-Yuga and the glorious beginning of the White Age of Satya-Yuga. How majestic is the image of the Kalki Avatar upon the white steed! With great yearning, the far-off Oirot awaits the White Burkhan. Our Old Believers who heroically go in quest of the White Waters of the Himalayas make this difficult journey only in the name of the future. In the very same name of the luminous future, the lama, with tears, tells us of the treasures of the mighty Rigden-jyepo who will annihilate evil and reestablish justice. The conquests of Gessar Khan led toward the future. Each New Year, the Chinese lights his candles and prays to the Lord of the Future. And in Isfahan, the white steed is kept saddled for the Great Coming. If you want to contact the best of humanity, speak with the people of the future, of that to which the human mind aspires even in the far-off desert. A special heart-filled solemnity pervades these strivings toward the transfiguration of the world.

In these darkest times, in the suffocating void of thought, the encouraging voice about the Great Advent, about the New Era, about the time when humanity will be able to wisely and inspiringly realize its destined possibilities, resounds with evocative force. Each person interprets this Radiant Age in his own way, but in one thing all are alike—they interpret it with the language of the heart. This is not accidental. On the contrary, it is just the opposite; it proceeds from all directions to the one because in every human heart, in the entire human kingdom, there is but one and the same striving to Bliss.

All are laboring to reunite these scattered drops of Mercury, if they are not too heavy with oil and not covered with dust. What an example there is in such a simple act as the outer soiling of a drop of Mercury, where one can still see the trembling of the inner substance beneath a polluted surface. It has become soiled through outer contact and thus has been isolated from the universal consciousness. The path back to the body of union is anticipated, but if the surface is not soiled, with what impetuous force these scattered drops fuse again with their primary source! And you can no longer identify them, nor will you distinguish the small particle which was assimilated by the whole. But it lives: It, the drop, exists in It, the Great. The force of all-union joined it and forged it to the universal. All teachings know this universal body under various names.

In the most unexpected manifestations we meet with these all-unifying signs. In the posthumous writings of the Elders of the desert, unexpected indications about the Himalayas were sometimes found. These writings, mandalas and other extraordinary signs arouse one's amazement and astonishment. But when the lama from the faroff mountain monastery was asked about it, he smiles and says: "Above all divisions, there exists one great unity, accessible only to a few."

Thus the trends of thought of the seemingly distant human individualities are merged. In these highest signs denial and condemnation are erased—the most hideous aspects which obscure the light of the heart. Often in our present day, we invent special expressions for the ancient understanding. We say pensively, "He understands psychology." This means in essence that he does not deny and does not condone his ignorance. We say, "He is practical and knows life," which means in essence that he does not condemn and thus does not set obstacles for himself. We say, "He knows the source," which means he does not disparage because he knows just how harmful each disparagement is.

In *Resurrection in the Flesh*, N. O. Lossky cites: "A worker who sets himself in opposition to the strivings of all other workers is in a state of isolation from them; he dooms himself to utilizing only his own creative force; hence, he is capable of producing only the most elementary actions, such as repulsion. The release from such impoverishment of life is reached by way of evolution which creates higher and higher steps of concrete Oneness.

"The members of the heavenly kingdom, not entering into a state of resistance, do not commit any acts of repulsion in space. Consequently, they do not have a material body; their transfigured body consists only of manifestations which are luminous, sonorous, warm, etc., but which do not exclude each other, and though egoistically separate, unique egos, they are capable of interpenetration with others. Having attained a concrete Oneness, which means having absorbed both the strivings of each other and the tasks of Divine Wisdom, they collectively create the Kingdom of perfect Beauty and all-manifesting Good. And they so create their bodies that, being mutually interpenetrating, they are not in possession of one personality but serve all—complementing each other, and forming individual omni-entities which are organs of the all-embracing wholeness of the Heavenly Kingdom. The free and loving unanimity of the members of the Heavenly Kingdom is so great that they all build, one many say, 'One body and one spirit'."

The significance of super-spaciousness is well expressed in the writings of the Father of the Church, the Holy Gregory of Nyssa. "The soul is not confined to spatial limitation," he says, "therefore for the spiritual essence, no great difficulty is involved in pervading each of the elements, with which, at some time, it has come into union during integration, since it is not divided by the contrariness of the elements; the spiritual and dimensionless essence is not affected by the consequence of distance. The friendly connection and acquaintance with the former parts of the body is forever retained in the soul."

To whom, then, will the words of our famous contemporary philosopher be especially clear? Certainly, a high lama will express a hearty response as well as benevolent understanding for them. Moreover, in his realistic metaphysics he will find a corresponding substantiation for them, and with elation he will join the discussion about the spirit. In other words, this constitutes his striving. The lama will recognize the universal body as Darmakaya. The highest communion of the representative of spirit he will call Dorjepundok. And he will do it not in the spirit of argument, but rather in that benevolent communion by which all boundaries are so easily erased.

In the East, they also understand Metalnikoff's idea of the immortality of the cell unit. The idea of unity, indivisibility, indestructibility is appreciated. The one who understands Dharma can also speak of immortality. With benevolence, they understand de Broglie, Millikan, Raman and Einstein. The main thing is that there must be a language of approach. For mutual understanding, one must know the inner and outer languages. One must know not only the outer hieroglyph; one must know the derivation of the sign, the evolution of the symbol, so that an incomprehensible exterior should not become a new barrier.

Is it then so difficult to unite in Bliss? One person may consider the sanctity of the Ganges to be superstition, but the true scholar will give its due to the wisdom of the people. It is truly beautiful to contact the facts and foundations of the people's wisdom. The waters of the Ganges are revered as sacred. And it is astounding that the countless multitudes of swarming people do not contaminate each other in the waters of the sacred river in Benares. But in addition to faith and to psychic protection, nature adds one more precious factor. Only recently it was discovered that special bacteria exist in the water of the Ganges that destroy other nests of contamination. The old knowledge manifests here its firm foundation.

All signs of unity are touching. The Buddhists see the icon of Saint Josav, the Hindu Prince, and wish to have a copy of it. The lamas see a fresco of Nardo Diccione in the Pisa Campo Santo and begin to explain its contents and the significance of the painted symbols. And when you read to them about Saint Josav from the *Golden Legend* they smile cordially. And in this smile is the same benevolence and inclusion which made room for Aristotle on the portals of the Cathedral of Chartres, together with the Saints and Prophets; and also the images of the Greek Philosopher in the frescoes of the churches of Bukovina. The image of the Moslem Akbar is in a Hindu temple; Lao Tse and Confucius are in an aureole of Catholic saints. All the black Madonnas and Rockamadura are from Negro soil. And King Solomon is in the Greek Orthodox Church of Abyssinia. If only one does not close one's eyes intentionally, a multitude of benevolent facts will flow in. Verily, following the statement of Origen, "We see with the eyes of the heart."

And it is not only ancient Chartres and Bukovina that revere the great Philosophers upon their portals. The newspapers of New York thus communicate the news about Riverside Church: "Confucius, Buddha and Mohammed, together with Christ, are modeled on the portals of the Church. The new era of religious tolerance is expressively symbolized in the images, where great scientists and philosophers, many of whom in their time were condemned for heresy, occupy a place together with saints, angels and leaders of religions—Moses is shoulder to shoulder with Confucius; after Buddha and Mohammed follow Origen, St. Francis of Assisi, Dante, Pythagoras, Plato, Socrates, Aristotle, St. Thomas Aquinas, Spinoza, Archimedes— Together with Dr. Fosdick who gave this testimony of his broad thinking, another representative of free thought, Dr. Holmes, has announced in a sermon that the temples of the future will represent the synthesis of all the great religions of the world."

Similarly speak the sermons of Dr. Guthrie in one of the oldest churches in New York, St. Marks-in-the Bowery. All recollect his Buddha day and as well as days devoted to other leaders of religious thought. The new temple of the Episcopal Church on Park Avenue, under the leadership of the eminent minister, Dr. Norwood, strives toward the same blissful synthesis.

If a venerable Moslem affirms that the Tomb of Christ

is in Srinagar, and begins in the most devout manner to enumerate the traditions and cures which have taken place near this Tomb, one cannot reprove him, for he speaks with the most benevolent intentions. Likewise, you will not object when in Kashgar they speak with conviction about the Tomb of the Holy Virgin being in the Miriam Mazar. Neither will you protest when they speak to you of Elijah, the Prophet, in the upper Indus, for first of all you feel their benevolence, and secondly, there is nothing of substance to contradict. Let us regard with care these benevolent signs of unification.

Or will you in wrath speak against the throne of King Solomon in Srinagar? On the contrary, you will rejoice that the thrones are many in Asia and according to the legends, the wise King Solomon flies even now above the vistas of Asia on his flying carpet. You will rejoice and remember the Amos Society in New York and its broad, benevolent aims.

There is a special joy when you hear the great names of Messiah, Maitreya, Muntazaar, united and pronounced in the same place with the same benevolent reverence and unifying signs.

Let us remember the touching Tibetan legend about the origin of many sanctuaries, and let us especially remember this now, when these benevolent signs do not bind us with the fetters of the past, but impel us toward the future.

And what is the invocation by the wise Apostle Paul when he writes to all ends of the world, to the Romans, the Hebrews, the Corinthians, the Ephesians and the Galatians: "Purge out therefore the old leaven, that you may be as new." "Therefore, let us keep the feast not with the old leaven." "He that is weak in faith receive ye, but not to doubtful disputations." "For one believeth that he may eat all things; another who is weak eateth herbs."

"Let us therefore follow after the things which make for peace and things wherewith one may edify another."

"Every man's work shall be revealed; for the day shall

declare it, because it shall be revealed by fire, and the fire shall try every man's work of what sort it is."

"When they shall say, 'Peace and Safety', then sudden destruction cometh upon them."

"Quench not the Spirit."

"Let us therefore cast off the works of darkness, and let us put on the armor of light."

"Attain love, be zealous of spiritual gifts."

"To write the same things to you, to me indeed is not grievous, but for you it is safe."

What is the command and prayer of spiritual reunion? For the future, the armor of light is needed. Isaiah, not only deploring the past, but in zeal for the future, also gave his forewarning with the ominous words: "Maher—Shelah—Ash—Baz."

Not for the past, but for the future traveler did Akbar plant the young trees along the roads of India.

What can be worse than to remove something and leave the site empty? Says Sloto Ust, "And when the soul diverts from love, then its mental gaze is clouded."

"Verily, most precious are the unifying signs! We do not forget the words of Vivekananda about Christ: "If I had met Christ during my life, I would have washed his feet with the blood of my heart." Are there many Christians who have in their hearts the same vital and uplifted feeling? And can one forget the words of the same Vivekananda when he asked the Chicago World Parliament Religions: "If you consider your teaching so supreme, why then do you not follow its covenants?"

Can one forget the fact that once when a Christian church was in an impoverished condition and was threatened with being sold at an auction, Jews spontaneously and voluntarily bought the Christian sanctuary and returned it to the bosom of the Metropolite E. who will affirm this.

It is not in the name of bliss that the Rabbi Kabbalist tells you: "You are also Israel if you search for light." And will you not smile benevolently at the Namtar narrated by the Central Asiatic Bakshi, concerning the miracles of the

[154]

great Issa-Christ? And will you not listen, after midnight in Kashmir to the glorification of Christ from the lips of the Moslem choir, accompanied by sitars and fantastic drums? Also I recollect all the reverential and deeply touching words of the Moslems of Sinkiang about Issa the Great and the Best.

Or if we take a book of the Reverend James Robson, *Christ in Islam,* instead of hostile signs whispered in ignorance we will see innumerable examples of heartfelt understanding and benevolence. The Old Believer sings the verses about Buddha. The New Testament is also placed among the sacred books in the suburgans. The Dravidian reads Thomas à Kempis' *Imitation of Christ.* The Moslem in Central Asia speaks of the holy bells beyond the mountain which are heard at dawn by the Holy Ones. Why does the Moslem need bells? It is simply a need for the call of benevolence. To the universal White Waters, the Siberian Old Believers are journeying in pilgrimage.

Let us remember all the sayings of all ages and peoples about the Holy People. The narrator does not even know about whom he speaks, whether of Christians, Buddhists, Moslems or Confucianists. He knows only of the benevolence of the achievements of these Holy Peoples. They, these Holy Ones, radiate an unearthly light; they fly; they hear at a distance of six months' journey; they cure; they self-sacrificingly share their last possession; they dispel darkness and untiringly create bliss upon their paths. Similarly speak the Old Believers and Mongols, Jews and Moslems, and Persians and Hindus.... the Saints become pan-human, they belong to the whole world in the true evolution of humanity. Everything contains light. The Chalice of Grail is above all bliss. The divine Sophia, the all-mightiest wisdom soars above the whole world.

Curses lead only to darkness. Not by wrath, not by succumbing, but only upon the blessed milestones can one cross the tempestuous ocean.

Here are the words from the Koran:

"O peoples of the earth, throw off all ties whatsoever,

if you desire to reach the Encampment prepared for you by God.

"Maybe then it will be possible to force the people to run away from the condition of apathy in which their soul exists, toward the Nest of Unity and Knowledge; then will they drink the water of eternal Guidance." "That is the holy and eternal lot, the heritage of pure souls at the divine Table."

This is from the Kabalah, from the great Shambatyon.

Eldad Ha-Dani describes the River Shambatyon, which united the children of Moses, as a stronghold of spiritual unification. The Moslem writers, Ibn-Fakich and Kasvini related how once the Prophet asked the Archangel Gabriel to carry him over into the site of the 'Children of Moses'—Banu Mussa—the land of the righteous ones. Gelilot Herez Israel relates Shambatyon to the sacred river of India which has healing properties. Healing unifications!

Let us not imagine that these ideas about unity are held only by all-encompassing innovators who shame dogma. The Orthodox and Roman Catholic churches constantly pray for the reunion of the churches, for a time of peace. This hope for the most spiritual, the most heartfelt unification, is not only dogma; it is the most life-creating, benevolent principle. And after this external reunion they hope for an era of peace. From the church pulpits we are carried into endless conferences for peace which also, each in turn, with more or less success, dream of peaceful times. Upon this spirit, the inner hope of all mankind is united. Both the most degenerate and the most striving ones are yearning for the days of peace and most splendid reunion. In the depths of the heart we understand that persecution, revilement and curses only lead to horror, division and pettiness. They lead us to subtle falsehood and vile hypocrisy.

Over the bridge will come the Messiah. The Kabbalists know of this unifying symbol. Upon a white horse comes the Great Rider with a comet as a sword of light in His hand. A distinguished Abyssinian says: "We have an ancient legend that says when the Savior of the World shall come, He shall pass over a stone bridge. Seven know of His coming, and when they see the Light, they shall fall down to earth and bow before it."

Is it accidental that the coming of the Messiah takes place over a bridge? What symbol is more appropriate for the thought of unity, of reunion? Already Maitreya is seated not in Eastern posture but in Western, with lowered feet, ready for the advent.... "Verily, never has the time been as short as ours." "The time is intense." "The time is short." "The time is close," the peoples exclaim in varied tongues, trembling with expectancy, gathering the highest symbols around their homes.

Why are these times of peace so necessary to humankind? Every heart knows that an era of peace is necessary for knowledge and construction. Hostile periods have brought on the material and spiritual crash. The human heart also knows this. Periods of hostility have created the unrest of unemployment, through which the worthiest striving towards the betterment of quality has been lost. Periods of hostility have resulted in numerous mediocrities, and in those atrocities that come from the absence of quality—in other words, in a spirit of savagery.

Very often conferences for peace invoke a pitying smile for the hypocrisy of people gathering to eliminate methods of destruction uncomfortable to them, in order to replace them with more subtle and modern ones.

But even among those who gather, there are always some who cherish the creative principle of peace. And these, not the bestial ones, like the drops of pure mercury, will still strive toward luminous unification, toward the great universal body. These striving ones can always find means of accord because by day and by night their hearts pray for unification. If this voice prevails, one is then able to realize the indestructible ennobling of the spirit which comes through the realization of culture. This is because each aspiring spirit in search of culture also knows the great sense of union and the time of peace in his heart.

He needs this sense of union, he needs this time of peace in order to open the gates of light. "Do not stand in the way".... "Do not obscure the sun," instructed Diogenes. He asked that light be not obscured, lest it give way to darkness.

Truly, the future will not tolerate sluggards. All has become dense. In the pressure of energies each moment of conscious labor is significant. Each banishment of egoism is significant. And the affirmation of cooperation is luminous.

The age of Maitreya was always indicated as the age of true cooperation. Natalie Rokotoff, in her remarkable book on Buddhism, thus characterizes the Age of Maitreya "The Future Buddha-Maitreya, as His name indicates, is the Buddha of compassion and love. This Bodhisattva, according to the power of His qualities, is often named Ajita the Invincible.

"It is interesting to note that the reverence of many Bodhisattvas was accepted and developed only in the school of Mahayana. Nevertheless the reverence of the one Bodhisattva-Maitreya, as a Successor chosen by Buddha Himself, is accepted also in Hinayana. Thus, the one Bodhisattva-Maitreya embraces the complete scope, becoming the personification of all aspirations of Buddhism.

"What qualities must a Bodhisattva possess? In the Teaching of Gautama Buddha and in the teaching of Bodhisattva-Maitreya, given by Him to Asanga according to tradition in the IVth century (Mahayana-Sutralamkara), the maximum development of energy, courage, patience, constancy of striving and fearlessness was first of all underlined. Energy is the basis of everything, as it alone contains all possibilities.

"Buddhas are eternally in action; immobility is unknown to them; like the eternal motion in space, the actions of the Sons of Conquerors manifest themselves in the world.

"Mighty, valiant, firm in His step, not rejecting the burden of achievement for the General Good.

"There are three joys of Bodhisattvas: the joy of giving; the joy of helping; and the joy of eternal perception. Patience always, in all and everywhere. The Sons of Buddhas, the Sons of Conquerors, Bodhisattvas in their active compassion are the Mothers to the All existing."

In giving the covenant of Shambhala, does not the East speak about the very same Light which is awaited in heartfelt benevolence and unity? "The Universal Eye of Shambhala carries benevolence to mankind. The Universal Eye of Shambhala is like the light upon mankind's path. The Universal Eye of Shambhala is that Star which has directed all seekers.

"For some, Shambhala is the truth; for others Shambhala is a Utopia. For some, the Lord of Shambhala is a Sage; for others the Lord of Shambhala is the manifestation of abundance. For some, the Lord of Shambhala is an adorned idol; for others, the Lord of Shambhala is the Guide of all planetary spirits. But We shall say—the Lord of Shambhala is a Fiery Mover of Life and of the Fire of the Mother of the World. His Breath glows with flame and His Heart burns with the fire of the Silvery Lotus. The Lord of Shambhala lives and breathes in the heart of the Sun!

"The Lord of Shambhala is the calling one and the called! The Lord of Shambhala is the sender of the arrow and the one who accepts all arrows! The Lord of Shambhala breathes with truth and affirms truth. The Lord of Shambhala is unconquerable and transforms destruction into construction. The Lord of Shambhala is the peak of the banner and the summit of light.

"Accept the Lord of Shambhala as the sign of life. I shall say thrice—of life; because Shambhala is a pledge of mankind's strivings. Our manifestation is the pledge of mankind's perfection. Our manifestation is the affirmed path to Infinity.

"The Lord of Shambhala manifests three ordinances to

humanity: The Teaching manifested by Maitreya calls the spirit into our creative world. The Teaching of Maitreya points out Infinity in Cosmos, in life, in achievements of spirit! The Teaching of Maitreya holds the knowledge of the cosmic fire, as the opening of the heart which contains the manifestation of the universe.

"The ancient legend affirming that the manifestation of Maitreya will evoke a resurrection of the spirit is correct. We will add that the resurrection of the spirit can precede the manifestation of the Coming, as the conscious acceptance of the Teaching of Lord Maitreya is verily resurrection!"

Does the East evoke the same spiritual strength, affirming the just necessity of the Hierarchy of Light?

"In the reconstruction of the world one may be sustained only by the affirmation of the New World. Manifestation of a decision can enter life only through the great understanding of universal regeneration, by the path of the great law of Hierarchy. Therefore those who seek the New World must strive toward the affirmation of the law of Hierarchy, which leads by the affirmed Hierarchy. Thus only may one establish balance in the world. Only a flaming, guiding Heart shall manifest salvation. Thus the world is in need of the affirmation of the law of Hierarchy.

"Therefore, according to the Law, Hierarchy is being affirmed in the shifting of countries and by the substitution by fire of everything which departs. Therefore it is so necessary to accept the law of Hierarchy, because without the chain, one cannot build the great ladder of ascent. Thus it is necessary to flamingly accept the affirmation of the grandeur of the law of Hierarchy.

"It is necessary to reiterate about Hierarchy. It is correct that the hierarchy of slavery is ended; nevertheless, the manifestation of a conscious Hierarchy is accomplished by the suffering of humanity. There is too much slavery in the world and each flame of consciousness is oppressed too greatly. Slavery and conscious Hierarchy are as night and day. Therefore do not hesitate to repeat—Conscious Hier-

archy, the Hierarchy of freedom, the Hierarchy of knowledge, the Hierarchy of light. Let those who do not know
the conception of the New World ridicule, because each
understanding of the New World is terrifying to them. Is
not Infinity horrible to them? Is not Hierarchy burden-
some to them? Being themselves ignorant despots, they do
not understand the creativeness of Hierarchy. Being themselves cowards, they are terrified before Hierarchy. Thus,
let us place in the balance the most needed understanding
of the approaching Great Age—Infinity and Hierarchy.

"One must accept Hierarchy as an evolutionary system.
For those spirits who have now outlived slavery, one may
repeat that Hierarchy absolutely differs from despotism.

"What path then is the most affirming one? The most
real way is the self-sacrifice of heroism. The most wondrous fire is the flame of the heart, imbued with love of the
Hierarchy. The heroic action of such a heart is affirmed
by service to the highest Hierarchy; therefore, the self-sacrifice of a subtle heart is wondrous. The spirit-creativeness
and independent activity of a sensitive servant imbues the
space with fire. Thus, verily harmonize the visible and the
invisible, the present and the future and the predestined
shall be fulfilled. Thus, the self-sacrifice of a subtle heart
imbues the world with flame.

"According to the construction of strata, the evolutionary spirit is being extended and the involutionary contract-
ed. One may observe this same fact, not only with individuals, but also with ideas. It is very instructive to discover
how ideas are born and accomplish their cycle; often, they
disappear completely. But if they are evolutionary, they
reappear in a broader way. One may study the spiral of
the roots of ideas for evolutionary thinking. The task of
gradual containment of an idea can give the progression
toward highest understanding.

"Labor, create benevolence, revere the Hierarchy of
Light—this, Our Covenant, one may inscribe even upon
the hand even of a newborn child. Thus simple is the

cause which leads to Light. In order to accept it, it is necessary only to have a pure heart.

"Hierarchy is a plane-metric cooperation. If anyone tries to explain it by the conventional understanding, he will only prove that his brain is as yet not ready for cooperation." Thus it is said.

Upon what, then, can we agree? Upon what basis may we forgive? Upon what shall we base our understanding? Upon what may we broaden ourselves? Upon what shall we avoid offense? Upon what may we move forward? Encircling all the spheres of Dante, we come to cooperation. Cooperation, compassion, are love itself. Ordained by all the hieroglyphs of the heart, love is the Mother of the World. Inexhaustible is creative love, which has conceived the Tribe of Holy People who know neither earth nor nation, who hasten upon wings of spirit to give succor, compassion, cooperation, who hasten in the name of bliss, who carry the drops of all-understanding, all-embracing bliss.

The world is hastening toward reconstruction. Human hearts are tired of wrath. In tumultuous labors they remember again about culture and the signs of Light, and they whisper to each other: "The future exists, that is why we have come here. Not for destruction, not for terror, but we pass here for mutual labor, for knowledge, for enlightenment. Let us then take hold of this Universal Light; let us achieve the transfiguration of the world, the preordained, the predestined."

All peoples know that the site of the holy men is on the mountains, upon the peaks. From the peaks comes revelation. The Rishis live in caves and upon the summits. There where the rivers find their sources, where the eternal ice has preserved the purity of whirlwinds, where the dust of meteorites carries a purifying armor from the distant worlds—there is a rising glow. There is directed the striving of the human spirit. The mountain paths attract one for their very difficulty. There the unexpected occurs. There the people's thought moves toward the Ultimate.

There each pass promises an unprecedented novelty, gives promise of the hewing of new facets of wondrous outline.

Upon the difficult paths, upon the dangerous mountain passes stand the images of Lord Maitreya of the Resplendent Future. Who made the effort to place them there? Whose was the labor? The traveler adds a little stone to the growing Mendang. Does one's heart ridicule this stone offered to the steps of the future? No. The difficult and dangerous path opens one's heart. One does not ridicule; but smiling in benevolence, one adds his stone also to the laying of the step toward the all-containing Light.

Long before dawn, under the stars, the entire neighboring mountain beyond the river is studded with tremendous roseate fires. They glide along, gathering into garlands, breaking into fragments, flashing out and disappearing, or moving back and forth to unite into one powerful flame. In the cold November air, we admire this Himalayan marvel which is familiar to all local inhabitants. In the morning you can ask the Guru about it and he, with sparkling eyes, speaks about the fires of Devitta; another whispers about the resplendent legion of Maitreya.

There are fires of earth. But here is a heavenly glow— Tibet knows "De-me," the fire of the deity and "Nam Bumpa," a fiery glow.

Over the snowy peaks of the Himalayas burns a bright glow, brighter than stars and the fantastic flashes of lightening. Who has kindled those pillars of light which march across the heavens? The polar and midnight regions are not near. The northern lights cannot glimmer in the Himalayas; not from the North come these pillars of light. They come from Shambhala, from the Tower of the Great Coming One.

MAITREYA COMES.

LEGEND OF THE STONE

THROUGH the desert I come—I bring the Chalice covered with the Shield. Within it is a treasure—the Gift of Orion. O Thou, Flame-bearer, remember Lob-Nor and spread Thy tents. Kuku-Nor—the steed hastens.

And in the Temple of Judea the Flame-bearer tarried not. And barely did Passedvan save It; with him It left the ruins of China behind. Reach not for the Stone, Lun; It will come of Itself if thou knowest to await It.

But by treason the servants of the temple usurped the Stone from the Rule of India to glorify a foreign land. Let the Mountain of Pride conceal for a while the Stone. Let the city of the Stone be glorified. But the path of the treasure is ordained. It is time for the Stone to return home.

When above the Chalice the flame shall coil in a ring, then My time approaches.

On the Island of Lanka lies the Stone hidden through the treachery of Ravana. It will depart beyond the sea. In its wake, as the tail of the comet, happiness is still ablaze, but not for long.

Let the hundred steps of China greet the Flame-bearer. But Passedvan bears away the Stone. And the sands transmit the Fire to the dauntless horseman, Timur. The great one approached the wall of amber and covered the field with his banners. "Let the Stone rest in the Temple until my return." But Life brought the miracle to the grandson. The way of the Stone turned westward.

Under the ground are assembled the religious fathers to analyze the nature of the Stone. "Why, when the Stone becomes dark, do the clouds gather? When the Stone feels heavy, blood is shed. When a star shines over the Stone, success follows. When the Stone creaks, the enemy approaches. When a dream of fire comes over the Stone, the world is convulsed. When the Stone is tranquil, walk courageously. But do not pour wine over the Stone. Burn only cedar-balsam over it. Carry the Stone in an ivory casket.

As one must be accustomed to heat and cold, so must one become accustomed to the radiance of the Stone. Each of the bearers of the Stone must abide with it tranquilly a while. The intoxication from Its rays is unseen but Its inner heat is mightier than radium. Unseen flows the Myrrh but the Stone rests visible upon the web of Its native land.

Amidst the breath of the steppe and the crystal resonance of the mountains, the spirit of the Stone marks the way of the banner. The miracle of Orion's rays is guiding the people.

To the tall Yutzakis and Karakorum Nor, the Teacher will lead the steeds. The manifestation is awaited.

Priestly knowledge of time immemorial has prepared men for the worthy reception of the Treasure. Long since have wisdom's laws revealed a day when a dual eclipse and the submersion of the sanctities would mark the new advent of the Stone. Let us in prayer await our destiny.

Oh, Stone, start hence over the sea. Let the bird bring to the ear the tiding—the Stone cometh.

In the darkness of the night darkly attired, the messenger noiselessly approaches to perceive how they await. Around the bend of the corner the tamed beast lies in wait, sniffing, groping with his paw; he is sent by the enemy. Who stirs behind the casement? What flies are swarming the place? Whence blows the whirlwind? But I walk firmly and securely; I am holding the Stone.

I am learning the prayer: "Forsake me not, my Lord. I have gathered all strength. Forsake me not for I come unto Thee."

On Mount Ararat lies the Fiery Stone. A knight of

Novgorod killed himself over the Stone because of unbelief. The great freedom of Novgorod proved the possession of the treasure but heresy diverted the fulfillment of the miracle.

The best relic of the power of the Stone is symbolized by the serpent's Stone—symbol of a wise possession.

The follower of night sought to regain possession of the Stone. But the Treasure was ever the token of Light. Not for long did sly rulers possess the Stone, being unaware that striving for right alone can rule the fire of the Stone.

Uroil Zena, Spirit of the air, bore the Stone to King Solomon. The Spirit proclaimed into the receptive ear: "By the will of the Lord of Powers I entrust unto thee the treasure of the Lord of Powers. I entrust thee the treasure of the world.

"So be it", said the King and carried the Stone into the Temple.

But the thought possessed him to carry part of the treasure on his person. Then the King summoned Ephraim, the goldsmith of the tribe of Judah; he bid him sever a part of the Stone and take pure silver and weld a ring and engrave upon the Stone the chalice of wisdom illumined with a flame. The king thought never to part with the treasure. But the Spirit said: "Not wisely didst thou violate the supreme A-Substance. It shall be sorely difficult for the sons of men to possess the Stone. And only those who are with thee can direct the Stone to righteousness. By a constellation shall I designate the way of the Stone."

Departed is the envoy to Khan Tamerlane. Uneasily lies the Stone at Otakuye. A guard of three banners must be dispatched. Upon camels, men are journeying. A pillar of sand obscures the sun. The elements conceal the travelers. Endlessly they wander. And the Kayuks turn their steeds homewards. At night, who shall safeguard the Stone?

The desert hid the strangers and with them, the Stone went to the south. Reflect, Khan, how to overtake the Stone righteously? Came sorrow and disease; the steed even loses its footing. To the worthy horsemen came the manifested Spirit: "Search not. Time alone will reveal they way."

Each Ulus sings its own song about the Stone.

Father Sulpicius beheld a vision. A white pillar of clouds appeared to him. From it issued a Voice: "Keep the Stone in the shrine brought from Rothenburg. Upon it are four squares in each, the sign M. The manifestation will be revealed when I shall pronounce the March of the Four eastward. Naught shall lessen the commandment. Yield to the destined hour. I shall assemble the warriors of My star. Whosoever are ordained to recognize the appointed time; they shall gather. This I attest by this hour, that the Stone is shaped like a human heart and within it is enshrined a resplendent crystal."

At these words, the pillar dispersed into blue sparks, casting Father Sulpicius into incomparable tremor.

Herein is the greater wonder, that the Stone which came from the East has the shape of a flat fruit or heart, oblong in form. Upon the shrine the foretold letters were found. Unknown is their meaning.

The ruler Kurnovoo, laden with gold, received from Tazlavoo the dark Stone containing the crystal of life. And over the gold the Ruler wore the Stone.

Out of the book of Tristan, called Lun:

"When the Son of the Sun descended upon earth to teach mankind, there fell from heaven a Shield which bore the power of the world. In the center of the Shield, between the three distinct marks, were signs of silver predicting events under the rays of the Sun. The sudden darkening of the Sun threw into despair the Son of the Sun and he dropped and shattered the Shield; for ominous was the constellation. But the power remained in the central fragment—there the ray of the Sun touched.

"It is said that King Solomon severed the central portion of the Stone for his ring. The legend of our priests also tells of the shattered shield of the Sun. It is a most grievous error to deny the Stone.

"Verily, I myself have seen this fragment of the world—I

recall the shape—the length of my little finger—of grayish luster like a dried fruit. Even the signs I remember but did not understand them.

"Truly I myself have seen the Stone and I shall find It. It is said that the Stone comes of Itself; It cannot be taken. If so, I shall await It. For Its sake, I shall take myself to the desert until the end of my days."

Remember, Lun, you decided to await It.

When the Stone was lost from the Rule of India, his wife said: "We find It again. The courageous one demandeth a bow, himself to mark down the bird."

When the Emperor of China possessed the treasure of the sun, he erected for It a turquoise temple of the color of the azure sky. When the little princes with the bride peered behind the door for a long time, the Emperor said: The fox is leading you, You feel the Joy of the world.

Remember the iron crown of the Longbards: that, too, is a trace of the Stone. Not long did the Stone rest near the Mountain of Pride. Many are the envoys from the East. The camels bring the Stone to Tibet. Across the desert they carry It and with It a new power. And Its last flight to the West lighted up an unheard-of kingdom of an unsuccessful union of western nations.

In each ray of the East, they already seek the Stone. The Time will come; the dates will be fulfilled. Designated is the ordained way when, of Itself , the Stone will come from the West.

We affirm to await and understand the way of the Stone. We affirm to understand the predestined carriers of the Stone who go homewards.

The ship is ready.

The New Country shall go forth to meet the seven stars under the sign of three stars which sent the Stone to the world. Prepared is the Treasure and the enemy shall not take the Shield covered with gold.

AWAIT THE STONE.

SACRED SIGNS

WE do not know. But they know.
The stones know. Even trees
Know.
And they remember.
They remember who named the mountains
And rivers,
Who constructed the former
Cities.
Who gave the names
To the immemorial countries—
Words unknown to us—
They are filled with meaning!
Everything is filled with achievements.
Everywhere
Heroes passed "To know"—
Is a sweet word. "To remember"—
Is a terrible word. To know and
To remember, to remember and to know
Means—to have faith.

Airships were flying.
Came pouring a liquid fire. Came flashing
The spark of life and death.
By the might of spirit stony masses
Ascended.
A wondrous blade was forged.
Scriptures guarded wise secrets.
And again all is revealed.
All new.
Fairy tale—legend—

Have become life. And we live again.
And again we shall change.
And again
We shall touch the earth.
The great "Today" shall be dimmed
Tomorrow.
But sacred Signs
Will appear. Then
When needed.
They will be unperceived. Who knows?
But they will create Life.
And where are
    The Sacred Signs?

(From Russian)

CPSIA information can be obtained
at www.ICGtesting.com
Printed in the USA
LVHW020737150721
692768LV00009B/372

9 781947 016149